KNOWLEDGE ENGINEERING
FOR INFORMATION SYSTEMS

THE McGRAW-HILL INTERNATIONAL SERIES IN SOFTWARE ENGINEERING

Consulting Editor

Professor D. Ince
The Open University

Other titles in this series

Portable Modula-2 Programming	Woodman, Griffiths, Souter and Davies
SSADM: A Practical Approach	Ashworth and Goodland
Software Engineering: Analysis and Design	Easteal and Davies
Introduction To Compiling Techniques: A First Course Using ANSI C, LEX and YACC	Bennett
An Introduction to Program Design	Sargent
Object Oriented Databases: Applications in Software Engineering	Brown
Object Oriented Software Engineering with C++	Ince
Expert Database Systems: A Gentle Introduction	Beynon-Davies
Practical Formal Methods with VDM	Andrews and Ince
SSADM Version 4: A User's Guide	Eva
Introduction to VDM	Woodman and Heal
A Structured Approach to Systems Development	Heap, Stanway and Windsor
Rapid Information Systems Development	Bell and Wood-Harper
Software Engineering Environments	Brown, Earl and McDermid
Introduction to Software Project Management	Ince, Sharp and Woodman
Systems Construction and Analysis: A Mathematical and Logical Framework	Fenton and Hill
Software Systems Development: A Gentle Introduction	Britton and Doake
Introduction to VDM	Woodman and Heal
An Introduction to SSADM Version 4	Ashworth and Slater
SSADM V4 A Project Manager's Handbook	Hammer

KNOWLEDGE ENGINEERING FOR INFORMATION SYSTEMS

Paul Beynon-Davies
University of Glamorgan

McGRAW-HILL BOOK COMPANY

London · New York · St Louis · San Francisco · Auckland · Bogotá · Caracas · Hamburg
Lisbon · Madrid · Mexico · Milan · Montreal · New Delhi · Panama · Paris · San Juan
São Paulo · Singapore · Sydney · Tokyo · Toronto

Published by
McGRAW-HILL Book Company Europe
Shoppenhangers Road, Maidenhead, Berkshire, SL6 2QL, England
Telephone 0628 23432
Fax 0628 770224

British Library Cataloguing in Publication Data
Beynon-Davies, Paul
  Knowledge Engineering for Information Systems.—
(McGraw-Hill International Series in Software
Engineering)
I. Title   II. Series
005.1
ISBN 0-07-707586-2

Library of Congress Cataloging-in-Publication Data
Beynon-Davies, Paul
   Knowledge Engineering for Information Systems/Paul Beynon
-Davies.
        p.   cm. -- (The McGraw-Hill international series in software
engineering)
Includes bibliographical references and index.
ISBN 0-07-707586-2
   1. Expert systems (Computer science) 2. Information storage and
retrieval systems.   I. Title   II. Series
QA76.76.E95B48   1992   92-23875
006.3'3--dc20

12345 TL 96543

Typeset by Goodfellow & Egan Phototypesetting Ltd, Cambridge
and printed and bound at Thomson Litho, East Kilbride

For my children: Rhydian, Ceri and Rhiannon

CONTENTS

PREFACE

Knowledge engineering is conventionally portrayed as a distinct, and somewhat remote, discipline from the more established disciplines of information systems building – information engineering and software engineering. This distinct portrait is drawn in a number of ways. For instance:

1. The theory and, to a large extent, the practice of knowledge engineering is largely the product of the academic world. It is only comparatively recently that knowledge engineering has been successfully applied within the commercial domain. Even now, however, the adoption of knowledge engineering principles and products has been very slow to take off.
2. Expert systems, probably the most successful commercial product of knowledge engineering to date, have been slow to find a place for themselves within conventional information systems. Most contemporary expert systems are standalone in nature. That is, such systems make few if any connections to other information system components.
3. The subject matter of knowledge engineering is still held to be fundamentally different in nature from the subject matter of software or information engineering. As a consequence, the process of engineering knowledge is held by many to be fundamentally different from the process of engineering software or information.

The main aim of this work is to challenge some of these widely held opinions. This challenge is made on a number of different fronts:

1. The author is firmly of the opinion that the distinction between knowledge engineering, software engineering and information engineering has been overdone. In other words, knowledge engineering has much to offer software and information engineering, and vice versa.
2. This integrative emphasis emerges in its most concrete form in the book's discussion of the process of building knowledge base systems. It will demonstrate, for instance, how a number of techniques presently used within the context of software and information engineering practice can be adapted to the needs of knowledge engineering.
3. A major objective of the current work is to demonstrate the practical application of

knowledge base systems to commerce and industry. This primarily means basing the case material around the application of expert systems and expert database systems to commercially-oriented projects.

4. The book highlights the way in which an expert system can form a central part of a larger information system. In particular, it demonstrates how expert systems can access data from large corporate databases, and be called from and make calls to other more conventional information system components.

5. The main aim of the work is to propose a framework for synthesizing the methods, tools, and techniques of knowledge engineering with the methods, tools and techniques of conventional information systems work. The synthesis is based around an analysis of information, information systems and consequently the place of knowledge base systems within organizations.

In summary, the present work is designed to form a companion volume to *Expert Database Systems: A Gentle Introduction*, McGraw-Hill, London (1991). *Expert Database Systems* described some of the major themes of convergence in modern day computing from an architectural point of view; that is, the way in which artificial intelligence and information systems work is contributing to a newer level of software. The present volume examines this convergence in a methodological sense. We wish to highlight the way in which the information and software engineers of today will need to be the knowledge engineers of tomorrow.

1

KNOWLEDGE ENGINEERING

1.1 INTRODUCTION

In a sense, the attempt to engineer knowledge is an ancient endeavour. The word 'knowledge' is derived from the ancient Greek word '*gignoskein*' which roughly translated means 'to decide upon, determine, or decree'. Epistemology, or the philosophical theory of knowledge, is at least as old as the term itself, and knowledge, or the problem of knowledge, has been of intensive interest to sociologists and psychologists for a number of centuries.

With the development of the discipline of artificial intelligence (AI), the emphasis has changed in modern times from a consideration of philosophical universals and social context to the problems of representation. In a sense, this is not really a change of emphasis, but a re-emphasis of the traditional concern with the problem of formalizing knowledge.

Contemporary knowledge engineering is therefore a computational exercise. It is the discipline devoted to building knowledge base systems, i.e. computing systems that utilize some representation of knowledge. The present chapter is devoted to expanding upon this initial definition for the term *knowledge engineering*. It discusses some of the basic terms that have achieved some prominence in the field, and uses this discussion to provide pointers for the chapters that follow.

We shall, however, return to a social and philosophical perspective on knowledge in Chapter 12 and discuss some of the implications of a modern critique of AI.

1.2 A BRIEF HISTORY OF KNOWLEDGE ENGINEERING

Artificial intelligence gained a name and an area of focus at the Dartmouth Conference in the summer of 1956 (McCorduck, 1979). The first period of AI research stimulated by this conference was dominated by the belief that a few general problem-solving strategies implemented on a computer could produce expert level performance in a particular domain. As such research developed, it was soon realized that such general-purpose mechanisms were too weak to solve most complex problems. In reaction to these limitations, researchers began to concentrate on more narrowly defined problems. By the mid-1970s, a number of so-called expert systems had begun to emerge. In 1977, Edward Feigenbaum presented the key insight into the power of the expert systems approach (Feigenbaum, 1977). He maintained that the power of an expert system derives not from the particular formalisms and inference mechanisms it uses, but from the knowledge it possesses. Knowledge, and not problem-solving strategy, is the important thing. It is for this reason that an expert system is often referred to as one, very successful, example of a knowledge base system.

Below we describe briefly some of the most important expert systems in the history of knowledge engineering.

1.2.1 DENDRAL

DENDRAL and META-DENDRAL were developed by a large research group at Stanford University. Both systems were concerned with various aspects of the elucidation of the structure of compounds in organic chemistry. The project was initiated in 1965 with the specific objective of providing computer support for professional chemists who were not necessarily experts in particular analytical techniques. Moreover, such was its success that it inspired the development of the whole expert systems area (Lindsay *et al.*, 1980).

1.2.2 MACSYMA

MACSYMA is an expert system which was developed at the Massachusetts Institute of Technology for symbolic mathematics. It performs differential and integral calculus symbolically and excels at simplifying symbolic expressions. Designed for use by mathematical researchers and physicists worldwide, it contains hundreds of pieces of knowledge elicited from experts in applied mathematics (Martin and Fateman, 1971).

1.2.3 MYCIN

MYCIN was developed at Stanford University to provide consultative advice on the diagnosis and treatment of infectious diseases. Its knowledge consists of approximately 4000 rules that relate possible conditions to associated conclusions (see Chapter 3). A panel of experts evaluated MYCIN's performance against medical experts in its particular specialism, and judged its performance at least as good (Shortliffe, 1976).

1.2.4 PROSPECTOR

MYCIN's use of IF-THEN rules (see Chapter 3) stimulated a variety of related systems. PROSPECTOR, a system developed by Stanford Research Institute in association with geological consultants and the US geological survey, was originally developed to help geologists working on problems of hard-rock mineral exploitation. It made headline news in 1982 when it was given the same field study data about a region of Washington State as that given to experts in a mining company. The system concluded that there were deposits of molybdenum over a wide area. The experts initially disagreed. When exploratory drilling was undertaken, however, PROSPECTOR was proved right (Duda and Gaschnig, 1981).

1.2.5 HEARSAY

HEARSAY is a speech-understanding system developed at Carnegie-Mellon University. It was one of the first systems capable of understanding connected discourse from a 1000-word vocabulary. Although this performance is only equivalent to that accomplished by a 10-year-old child, many researchers believe that the ideas incorporated within HEARSAY will play an important role in the future development of expert systems (Erman *et al.*, 1980).

Most of the early expert systems, such as those described above, were academic research vehicles directed primarily at technical areas such as medical diagnosis. One effect of this has been to divert the early commercial exploitation of this technology into areas of a similar technical nature. Perhaps the most heavily publicized of such systems is DEC's R1 – an expert system built to configure VAX mainframes. The early applications in commerce were therefore primarily standalone systems in areas such as fault diagnosis or breakdown prediction.

The major problem with this approach is that expert systems and conventional information systems form islands of computing with little or no connection to each other. In recent years a number of developments have taken place which allow us to build bridges between these islands. In a similar vein to Beynon-Davies (1991), we identify the major thesis of this work as being that a large proportion of work on commercial information systems, including all non-trivial database applications, will benefit from the application of knowledge engineering principles and practices.

1.2.6 Knowledge engineering in Britain

In Britain the history of knowledge engineering has been a varied one. In 1973 an influential and highly damaging report, known as the Lighthill report, was produced for the principal British government agency for financing scientific research – the Science Research Council. This report was highly damning of AI and effectively decimated most of the AI research in Britain during the 1970s. A few determined centres of resistance, most notably at the University of Edinburgh, did survive, however.

One of the leading British proponents of expert systems was, and still is, Professor Donald Michie of the University of Edinburgh. During the 1970s Michie did much to alert the British computer industry to the pioneering work being carried out in the US on systems such as DENDRAL, MYCIN and PROSPECTOR.

The culmination of this effort was the formation of a British Computer Society specialist group on expert systems in the summer of 1980. This coincided with the announcement towards the end of 1981 of the Japanese Fifth Generation Computer Initiative (Feigenbaum and McCorduck, 1984). As a response to this, the British Government set up the Alvey Programme for Advanced Information Technology.

In the Alvey report, intelligent knowledge-based systems (IKBS) were identified as a major area in need of development. The Alvey Programme has funded numerous activities in many different areas. A particularly valuable innovation was the formation of a number of expert systems awareness clubs. Such clubs were made up of a number of organizations from both industry and academia with a common interest. A number of such awareness clubs are listed below:

- ALFEX (Alvey Financial Expert Systems Club)
- ARIES (Insurance Community Club)
- DAPES (Data Processing Expert Systems Club)
- TRACE (Transport and Travel Club)
- PLANIT (The Planning IKBS Club)

The current position is that a considerable number of British companies are now involved in some form of expert system development (Bramer, 1988). Most universities and polytechnics now appear to have expert systems projects, and most contemporary degree courses in computer science or computer studies offer AI and expert systems as part of their syllabus.

1.3 WHAT IS KNOWLEDGE?

We speak of engineering knowledge, but what is knowledge? As an initial definition we might define knowledge in the computational perspective as being 'the symbolic representation of aspects of some named universe of discourse' (Winston, 1984). Note the two assumptions of this definition:

1. We can symbolize knowledge. That is, it can be represented in some way. Hence, AI has often seen itself as being a discipline concerned with symbolic processing (Simon, 1969).
2. We understand that an area of knowledge, often referred to as a knowledge domain, can be named or referenced in some way.

Below we list some examples of commercial knowledge domains:

- Statutory sick pay
- Interpreting UK employment law
- Portfolio management
- Credit assessment
- Reordering stock
- Producing customer mailshots
- Planning production schedules

In Chapter 2 we discuss in more detail what we mean by knowledge, and make the comparison with data and information in conventional computing systems.

1.4 KNOWLEDGE REPRESENTATION AND KNOWLEDGE ELICITATION

In the next three sections we discuss three complementary ways of defining the discipline of knowledge engineering: in terms of major activities; in terms of key roles; and in terms of its major product.

It should be noted that there is no contemporary consensus as to the meaning of the term knowledge engineering. Any attempt to write about the subject must therefore contain a lot of personal definition. The present book is no different. Having said this, there is some form of agreement as to two major types of activity engaged in within knowledge engineering.

1. Knowledge elicitation (sometimes referred to as knowledge acquisition). The process of extracting knowledge from one or more experts in a particular domain.
2. Knowledge representation. Where knowledge is stored in a knowledge base in a form most appropriate for the given application.

Knowledge elicitation is a methodological issue. In the main, it concerns the whole process of interacting with people and documenting the results of this interaction. In contrast, knowledge representation is an implementation issue. It concerns the means of implementing the 'intelligence' involved in some particular domain in a computational medium.

Knowledge elicitation and representation are not independent processes, but intermingle throughout the entire life-cycle of a knowledge base system project. For the sake of presentation, however, some rough distinction has been made in this book. The first few chapters of the book concentrate on representational issues, and describe two of the major contemporary formalisms used for representing knowledge in a knowledge base system: rule-based systems and frame-based systems. The second, and major, half of the book concentrates on methodological issues. It discusses some of the traditional techniques used in the development of expert systems such as rapid prototyping, and makes the case for a more structured methodology for the development of knowledge base systems.

1.5 KNOWLEDGE ENGINEER AND DOMAIN EXPERT

It is traditional to indicate that there are two main roles involved in the knowledge engineering process:

1. Knowledge engineer. The person who implements the knowledge base system.
2. Domain expert. The person who provides the expertise on which the knowledge base system is modelled.

For those familiar with traditional software development, the knowledge engineer roughly corresponds to what we know as the analyst/programmer. In a similar manner, the domain expert may also be classed as the user, although this may not strictly be the case. The whole purpose of a knowledge base system, for instance, is usually to replicate the knowledge of a domain expert for use by other persons.

1.6 DEFINITION OF A KNOWLEDGE BASE SYSTEM

In practical terms, knowledge engineering is the discipline devoted to building knowledge base systems. *Knowledge base system* is a more encompassing term than expert system. There are knowledge base systems, such as natural language systems, which are not strictly expert systems. There are also expert systems which have had their functionality significantly enhanced via connections to more conventional software such as database systems. As we shall demonstrate, contemporary standalone expert systems have a limited application in commercial computing. In contrast, knowledge base systems have an enormous potential.

The term knowledge base system shall hopefully become clearer after reading the first few chapters of the book. In these introductory chapters, the aim has been to explain the concept with reference to conventional software. For this reason, we begin by discussing a very influential conventional computing model, namely the relational data model. Discussing this model first provides a fruitful basis for a number of important points made throughout the book.

For those in need of an initial definition, however, one is provided below. A knowledge base system is a set of resources designed to:

1. Represent and store knowledge.
2. Provide inferencing facilities.
3. Include a consistent user interface.
4. Incorporate means for connecting the system to conventional software.

Points 1 to 3 are relatively uncontroversial. Point 4 is something the author personally believes to be of primary importance.

Readers may have come across the terms 'intelligent knowledge-based system, and 'knowledge-based system'. It is tempting to delete the word 'intelligent' from the former term because of its value-laden nature. Knowledge base or knowledge-based systems are often described as being 'intelligent' in the sense that they attempt to simulate many of the activities which when undertaken by a human being are regarded as being instances of intelligence. This is clearly unsatisfactory, however, in the sense that the boundaries of intelligence are an ill-defined set of moving targets. The terms 'knowledge-based system' and 'knowledge base system' are less controversial. The term 'knowledge base system' is preferred in this work because it is more amenable to some of the connections we wish to make with database and information systems development.

1.7 FIRST AND SECOND ORDER KNOWLEDGE BASE SYSTEMS

The eventual aim of a knowledge base system is probably to represent all knowledge in one way. Many people, for instance, feel that the right direction is to represent knowledge in the form of some notation based in formal logic. As a stepping-stone in the direction of a full knowledge base system, however, other people are considering the integration of two pieces of existing software: a database management system (DBMS) and an expert system shell. The DBMS supports the conventional information processing; the expert system shell supports the rule-based processing.

This latter architecture we might call a first order knowledge base system (Beynon-Davies, 1991). In contrast, an architecture for a knowledge base system based on one consistent representation we shall call a second order knowledge base system. In this architecture, rules and facts are stored in one way, and are handled by one system, namely a knowledge base management system (KBMS). Primitive knowledge base systems of this form can already be built to a degree using object-oriented systems such as SMALLTALK, or the tools of logic programming, most notably PROLOG. Any major advances in this area, however, will probably only emerge with the development of specialized hardware more suited to the development of 'intelligent' software (Feigenbaum and McCorduck, 1984).

1.8 LEVELS OF CONVERGENCE

In *Expert Database Systems: A Gentle Introduction* we discussed the inherent imprecision associated with the term *expert database system*. A study of the literature reveals at least four different interpretations of the term defined by the intersection of larger and larger areas of computer science. In Fig. 1.1, these domains are portrayed as sets on a Venn diagram.

1. In its most limited sense, the term 'expert database system' can be defined as that endeavour which attempts to connect existing software tools, such as database management systems and expert system environments, to solve problems at the fringes of conventional information processing.
2. In another sense, the term is often used to describe the enhancement of data management systems with 'intelligent' software, or the enhancement of expert systems with more sophisticated data management facilities. Database systems are

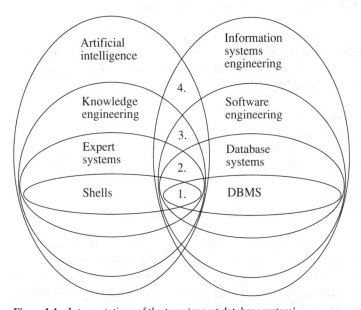

Figure 1.1 Interpretations of the term 'expert database system'.

increasingly looking to expert systems technology to provide a necessary inferencing capability. Expert systems need databases to store the large amounts of facts needed by commercial applications.

3. The term is also used to cover most of the advanced work in the database area. This is particularly true in a number of proposals for new database architectures such as semantic data models, object-oriented approaches and the application of logic to database work. In this sense we might define the field of expert database systems as the intersection of knowledge engineering with software engineering.

4. Perhaps the most encompassing, but probably most controversial, definition is any piece of software lying at the intersection of artificial intelligence work and information systems engineering work. Many of the most commercially successful offshoots of AI would fall into this category, including a growing number of computer-aided information systems engineering tools which incorporate some degree of 'intelligence'.

The definitions in 1 and 2 above relate primarily to architectural issues, particularly the distinction between first and second order knowledge base systems as described in Section 1.7. Beynon-Davies (1991) represents an attempt to introduce this architectural convergence.

Definitions 3 and 4 begin to relate to methodological issues, particularly the interaction of AI work with conventional information systems work. The present volume is devoted to introducing this ongoing methodological convergence.

1.9 COMMERCIAL KNOWLEDGE BASE SYSTEMS

The whole area of knowledge base systems has been gradually moving out of the academic and scientific arena into the commercial world. For instance, the following list of examples will give the reader some idea of existing applications in this area (Johnston, 1986; Bramer, 1988; Humpert and Holley, 1988).

1. Advice to employers on the dismissal of staff.
2. Provision of welfare benefits advice.
3. Construction of models and plans of marketing environments for consumer goods.
4. Assistance with personnel selection.
5. Company tax advice.
6. Assistance with office allocation.
7. Support for portfolio managers in recommending investment strategies.

Most of the systems described above are so-called standalone systems. By this we mean that such systems make little connection with other more conventional systems and work from a zero-base of information. In other words, the usual way of working of most presently available expert system products is by continually prompting the user for the information needed to come to a particular conclusion.

1.10 DATABASES TO KNOWLEDGE BASES

The coming of age of knowledge engineering will not cause the centre of gravity of computing to change substantially in most organizations. The net effect of the advent of knowledge engineering principles, techniques and methods will largely be to extend and probably formalize those parts of current database applications that are conventionally referred to as business rules.

Most current database technology distinguishes carefully between data, information and rules. Data is usually stored using a formalism such as the relational data model. Information is built into the application model by the specification of integrity constraints. Business rules are usually implemented as procedures written in some host language such as C or COBOL.

The coming of age of knowledge engineering promises to provide better facilities for handling business rules. Such facilities will greatly simplify the representation, storage and maintenance of business knowledge.

Whereas a large amount of literature has built up around methods for database development, the literature on knowledge base development is only beginning to emerge. This book is a personal attempt to provide an introduction to this emerging literature.

1.11 CONCLUSION

Expert systems, knowledge base systems and knowledge engineering have been subject to a phenomenon well known in the computing world over the last few years. This we might call the hype curve. In the mid-1980s expert systems were definitely on the upward swing of the hype curve. Expert systems were portrayed as the saviours of computing. Over the last couple of years, expert systems have begun to emerge onto the flat section of the curve. The strengths and limitations of expert systems are more clearly perceived. The place of expert systems within organizational computing is easier to see.

For knowledge engineering to take off as a commercial proposition, the mainstream of conventional data processing departments has to be turned on to knowledge base systems. This can only be done to a limited extent by the application of standalone systems to the fringes of conventional computing. What needs to be done is the employment of knowledge base software for the task of cleaning up the exceptions that conventional systems cannot handle. This means embedding knowledge base systems within conventional systems; allowing them to access databases and communicate their results to conventional programs written in languages such as C or COBOL.

It is the author's belief that such embedding is possible, and hence that knowledge base systems will form an important part of the information systems of the future. After reading this book it is hoped that the reader will come to the same conclusion.

1.12 RECALL EXERCISES

1. Define the computational view of knowledge.
2. Define artificial intelligence.

3. What is meant by knowledge engineering?
4. What is meant by a standalone expert system?
5. What is meant by a knowledge domain?
6. Distinguish between knowledge representation and knowledge elicitation.
7. Distinguish the role of knowledge engineer from that of domain expert.
8. What is meant by a first and second order knowledge base system?
9. Is an expert system a knowledge base system?
10. Describe some of the developments needed to make knowledge engineering a commercial proposition.

1.13 OPEN-ENDED EXERCISES

1. Philosophers define knowledge as justified true belief. How does this fit with the computational view of knowledge discussed in this chapter?
2. Sociologists have highlighted knowledge as a social construction, particularly its role as ideology. Radical social scientists point to the hegemony of ideology – the imposition of the ruling class's ideology as the dominant ideology in society. Discuss this conception of knowledge in the light of knowledge base systems work. Does this mean that knowledge base systems are artefacts of hegemory?
3. Why do you think that the concept of intelligence has been defined in this chapter as a moving target?
4. Philosophers have been studying the problem of knowledge for millenia. Is it therefore presumptious to assume that we currently have the means to engineer *knowledge*? Discuss.

REFERENCES

Beynon-Davies P. (1991). *Expert Database Systems: A Gentle Introduction*. McGraw-Hill, London.
Bramer M.A. (1988), Expert systems in business: a British perspective. *Expert Systems*, 5(2), 104–117.
Duda R.O. and Gaschnig J.G. (1981). Knowledge-based expert systems come of age. *Byte*, 6(9).
Erman L.D., Hayes-Roth F., Lesser V., and Reddy D. (1980). The HEARSAY-II speech understanding system: integrating knowledge to resolve uncertainty. *Computing Surveys*, 12 (2).
Feigenbaum E.A. (1977). The art of artificial intelligence: themes and case studies of knowledge engineering. *IJCAI*, 5, 1014–1029.
Feigenbaum E.A. and McCorduck P. (1984) *The 5th Generation: Artificial Intelligence and Japan's Computer Challenge to the World*. Michael Joseph, New York.
Humpert B. and Holley P. (1988). Expert systems in finance planning. *Expert Systems*, 5(2), 78–100.
Johnston R. (1986). Early applications get user approval. *Expert Systems User*, November.
Lindsay R.K., Buchanan B.G., Feigenbaum E.A. and Lederburg J. (1980). *Applications of Artificial Intelligence for Organic Chemistry: the DENDRAL Project*. McGraw-Hill, New York.
Martin W.A. and Fateman R.J. (1971). The MACSYMA system. *Proc. of 2nd Symposium on Symbolic and Algebraic Manipulation*, Los Angeles, 59–75.
McCorduck P. (1978). *Machines who think*. Freeman and Co, New York.
Shortliffe E.H. (1976). *Computer-Based Medical Consultations: MYCIN*. Elsevier, New York.
Simon H.A. (1969). *The Sciences of the Artificial*. MIT Press, Cambridge, MA.
Winston P.H. (1984). *Artificial Intelligence*. Addison-Wesley, Reading, MA.

2

INFORMATION, INFORMATION SYSTEMS AND ORGANIZATIONS

2.1 INTRODUCTION

Having defined knowledge engineering to be the discipline devoted to building knowledge base systems, it may seem somewhat strange to place the term 'information system' alongside the term 'knowledge engineering' in the title of this work. However, the intention of this association will become clear as we examine the related concepts of information and information system in this chapter.

The concept of information and its exploitation in information systems has been somewhat taken for granted in the contemporary practice of development. Information has been treated generally as a mystical fluid which emanates as a matter of course from the development of computerized information systems.

In recent years there has been a resurgence of interest in the philosophical and sociological underpinnings of information systems work. As such, a discipline of information systems is emerging which has boundaries with management, business studies, behavioural science, computing and many other areas (Backhouse et al., 1991). This work is fundamentally an attempt to discuss the overlap of information systems work with knowledge base systems and AI.

2.2 WHAT IS INFORMATION?

The concept of *information* is an extremely vague one open to many different interpretations (Stamper, 1985). One conception popular in the computing literature is that information results from the processing of data – the assembly, analysis or summarization of data. This conception of information as analogous to chemical

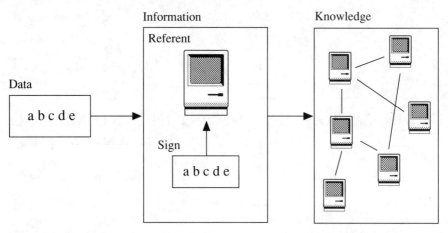

Figure 2.1 Data, information and knowledge.

distillation is useful but ignores the important place of human interpretation. In this section we shall define a workable definition of information based upon the distinction between data, information and knowledge. We shall elaborate on this definition in Chapter 3 when we consider the issue of knowledge and its representation. Here, we concentrate particularly on putting people back in the information picture.

Tsitchizris and Lochovsky usefully define information as being 'an increment of knowledge which can be inferred from data' (1982). Information therefore increases a person's knowledge of something. Note that this definition interrelates the concepts of data, information, knowledge and subject, as shown in Fig. 2.1:

1. Data are facts. A datum, a unit of data, is one or more symbols used to represent something.
2. Information is interpreted data. Information is data with attributed meaning in context.
3. Knowledge is derived from information by integrating information with existing knowledge.
4. Information is necessarily subjective. Information must always be set in the context of its recipient. The same data may be interpreted differently by different people depending on their existing knowledge.

Consider the string of symbols, 43. Taken together these symbols form a datum which is meaningless. To turn these symbols into information we have to supply a meaningful context. We have to interpret them. This might be supplying the context that they constitute an employee number, a person's age, or the quantity of a product sold. Information of this sort will contribute to our knowledge of a particular domain. It might add, for instance, to our understanding of the total number of products of a particular type sold, and might be included in some future decision-making on marketing policy.

Meaning triangle

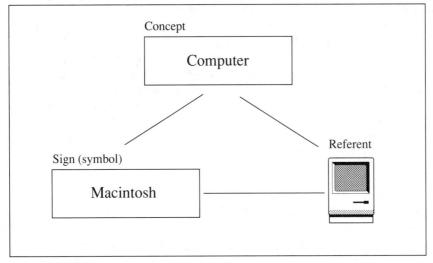

Figure 2.2 A meaning triangle.

2.3 SEMIOTICS

Liebenau and Backhouse (1990), following Stamper (1973, 1985), have usefully discussed the concept of information in terms of semiotics. Semiotics or semiology is the discipline which studies semiosis. Semiotics is the study of communication and understanding. Semiosis is the process by which communication and understanding occur.

Semiotics is not usually seen as an academic discipline. It is more accurately portrayed as a theoretical approach and its associated methods of analysis (O'Sullivan *et al.*, 1988). Stamper portrays semiotics as 'not so much a new subject as a regrouping of ideas from many disciplines having their own private jargons, and little intercommunication' (1973).

Semiotics is the study of signs. One of the most important categories of signs is the symbol. A symbol is a sign which requires a convention linking the signifier (the symbol) to that which it is representing (the signified or referent). The fundamental model of semiosis can be portrayed in terms of a meaning triangle (Sowa, 1984), as shown in Fig. 2.2. The left corner of the triangle is the symbol; the peak is the concept; and the right corner is the referent.

A given sign can be considered on a number of different levels:

1. Pragmatics. Signs in relation to human behaviour.
2. Semantics. How signs are related to the 'real' signs they signify.
3. Syntactics. The formal relations among signs.
4. Empirics. The statistical relations among sets of signs.

Pragmatics and semantics study the purpose and content of communication. Syntactics and empirics study the forms and means of communication. Pragmatics and semantics clearly impinge upon other disciplines such as sociology and politics. Syntactics and empirics impinge upon the domain of psychology and indeed even electronics.

Consider, for instance, a mail message transmitted on an office automation system. The mail message is something which exists within a social setting. It therefore exists within an environment of expectations, commitments and obligations. At the pragmatic level there must be some reason for sending the message which is presumably expressed in terms of the culture and context in which the information is used. At the semantic level the focus shifts to the subject matter of the message. At the syntactic level the language used to express the message is of concern. In so far as the communication takes place along electronic communication lines, issues such as bandwidths and other properties of signal transmission will be the concern of the empirics level.

2.4 WHAT IS AN INFORMATION SYSTEM?

The term *information system* is used in a number of different contexts in the literature. This section attempts to build a workable definition of the term and, in the process, introduces a number of important distinctions.

A system might be defined as a coherent set of interdependent components which exists for some purpose, has some stability, and can be usefully viewed as a whole. The class of systems to which computing is generally applied have been referred to as human activity systems (Checkland, 1980). Such systems consist of people, conventions and artefacts designed to serve human needs.

A high street branch of a British building society is clearly a human activity system. Staff of the branch are primarily involved in the activity of dealing with money transactions provided by customers. Customers pay money into building society accounts and withdraw money from such accounts. Other activities include advising customers on such financial matters as mortgages, pensions and investments.

Every human activity system will have one or more information systems. The purpose of these information systems is to manage the human activity system. Such information systems may be formal, informal, or technical.

> To understand an organisation we must recognise three layers corresponding to the formal, informal and technical levels at which culture is transmitted and behaviour determined. At the formal level are the explicitly recognised precepts of behaviour which may be a part of the wider culture in which the organisation operates; on the other hand they may be expressed in the rules, regulations and official structure of authority. At the informal level, an organisation will gradually evolve complex patterns of behaviour which are never formulated, but which must be learnt by newcomers. The informal culture will be vital to the effectiveness of the organisation; in some respects it may aid, and in others impede, the attainment of organisational objectives . . . At the technical level an organisation must be described in terms of its flows of messages about the transactions performed, plans made, problems investigated, and in terms of the data-processing activities necessary to accomplish organisational tasks (Stamper, 1973).

In terms of a building society branch, a technical information system will correspond to the links the branch has to the society's centralized accounts systems. A formal information system corresponding to the regulations and procedures appropriate to building society accounts will surround this system. Finally, an informal system of branch norms, expectations and practices for dealing with customers will surround the formal information system.

2.5 FORMAL INFORMATION SYSTEMS

The primary purpose for creating an organized information system is to serve real-world action. The provision of information in organizations is always linked to action: i.e. deciding to do things, accomplishing them, observing and recording the results and if necessary iteratively repeating this process. From the definition of information as data to which meaning has been attributed, and the objective of information systems as servers for action, a number of consequences follow:

1. Information systems are systems of signs. As a consequence, the boundary of information systems will always have to include the attribution of meaning, which is a uniquely human act. An information system will consist of both data manipulation and the attribution of meaning by humans.
2. The process of developing an information system requires explicit attention to the purposeful action which the information system is meant to serve. This involves understanding how the people in the organization conceptualize their world: how they attribute meaning, and how this meaning drives action.

For this reason, Checkland and others of the 'soft' systems school prefer to distinguish between technical systems built with the use of computers, which they portray merely as data manipulation systems, and true information systems which must contain a human component (Checkland and Scholes, 1990); this is demonstrated in Fig. 2.3. While this

Information system

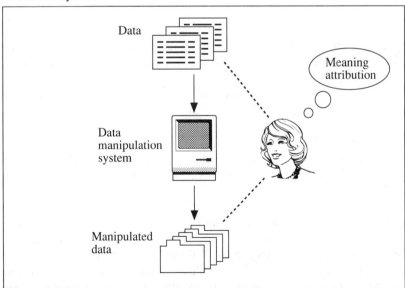

Figure 2.3 Definition of an information system according to the 'soft' systems school.

portrait is useful in buffeting the dominant 'technicist' ethos in the information systems development world, it does tend to ignore some of the ongoing developments which are attempting to make computing systems more adaptable by building in some of the elements of human interpretation (see Chapter 3).

2.6 THE IMPORTANCE OF INFORMAL INFORMATION SYSTEMS

On the morning of 27 October 1986 the new computerized price and dealing information system of the London stock market went down. Breakdowns and suspensions of trading occurred on the system for the following month. When an evaluation was conducted, the source of the problem proved to be a massive underestimation of the volume and timing of system usage. On the first day, everybody logged onto the system out of curiosity. Thereafter, regular massive early loading of the system was commonplace as dealers struggled to get their share prices right as early in the day as possible (Willcocks and Mason, 1987).

The analysis of the formal system of stock market information was done well given the constraints of a tight development schedule. The price and dealing information system (the technical system) was produced on time. However, the analysis of the informal system of share dealing was done badly.

The main importance of informal information systems is that they can be more robust than information systems established on formal and particularly technical grounds. An informal information system, because of its very nature, is likely to be better able to adapt to the changes in the external environment.

2.7 SEMI-FORMAL INFORMATION SYSTEMS

The potential of knowledge base systems for information systems work is manifold. For instance, knowledge base systems offer the possibility of extending the application of computing from the strictly formal to the boundaries of informal information systems. Knowledge base systems might be regarded as semi-formal information systems (Liebenau and Backhouse, 1990).

Following Lai *et al.* (1988), we might define a semi-formal information system as being a technical information system that:

1. Represents and processes information in formally specifiable ways.
2. Represents and processes information in ways that are not formally specifiable.
3. Allows the boundary between formal processing by computers and informal processing by people to be easily changed.

Without denying the important place of human interpretation in any information system, knowledge base systems offer the possibility of building much more meaningful mechanisms into technical information systems. Knowledge base technology offers a more flexible and adaptable framework for sign production and representation. The aim of knowledge engineering is not expressed here as an attempt to replicate human intelligence but as a means to augment it.

Some of the problems of the early stock market system discussed in Section 2.6 may have been alleviated with the application of knowledge base systems. One way in which this might have occurred is if 'intelligent' interfaces had been built to the central pricing system. Such an interface might adaptively build a profile of its user in terms of a general portfolio of shares of interest. Since the user would only be alerted if the value of important shares changed significantly, the loading on the system would have been likely to be far more uniform.

2.8 CORPORATE KNOWLEDGE

In Chapter 6 we shall discuss two interrelated methods for assessing the feasibility of knowledge base projects. In this section we discuss a useful model for understanding the place of knowledge base systems in organizational information systems.

In Fig. 2.4 we have superimposed the related concepts of data, information and knowledge on the classic pyramidal representation of organizational levels: the operational level, the administrative level and the strategic level.

Data, such as the number of products of a particular type sold to a particular customer, is produced at the operational level of a business. This data must be given a purpose by being processed by some formal or technical data manipulation system and interpreted by those persons making the day-to-day administrative decisions of the organization. Decisions such as the amount of stock to reorder are classic administrative decisions. Information produced at the administrative level must be incorporated into the strategic decision-making of the business. Although knowledge is used at the various levels within an organization, it is strategic knowledge which is probably the most important for an organization's survival. It is at this level that we can truly speak of corporate knowledge.

Most existing computerized information systems have been applied to the administrative levels of organizations. Some have migrated downwards to the operational level, but relatively few have migrated upwards to the strategic layer. This is probably because the information systems required at this level have to be much less formalized than those possible at the administrative and operational levels.

Semiformal information systems are most useful when we understand enough to formalise in a computer system some, but not all, of the knowledge relevant to acting in a given situation. Such systems are often useful in supporting individual work, and we believe they are especially important in cooperative work where there are some well-understood patterns of

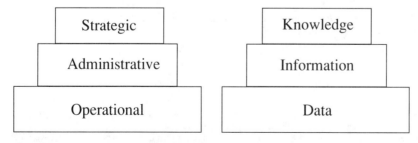

Figure 2.4   Pyramidal representation of data, information and knowledge.

behaviour and also a very large amount of other knowledge that is potentially relevant but difficult to specify (Lai *et al.*, 1988).

It is for this reason that we expect knowledge base systems to have their greatest impact on the strategic layer of organizational information (see Chapter 12).

2.9 CONCLUSION

Much of the work taking place in knowledge engineering has been caught up in the hype surrounding AI. AI in general, and knowledge engineering in particular, have been portrayed as the saviours of software development. This issue will be discussed in more detail in Chapter 5.

Like all hype, this portrayal contains at least an element of truth. AI and knowledge engineering are unlikely to be saviours. They are, however, in the words of Anderson (1991), 'disciplines which offer new modes of sign production'. In particular they offer new approaches to representing knowledge and consequently of building information systems. It is to this issue of knowledge representation that we now turn.

2.10 RECALL EXERCISES

1. Define the term 'information'.
2. What is meant by an information system?
3. What is semiotics and how is it applicable to information systems work?
4. Distinguish between formal, informal and technical information systems.
5. In what way are knowledge base systems semi-formal information systems?

2.11 OPEN-ENDED EXERCISES

1. Knowledge is power. Discuss the use of knowledge base systems as a tool in organizational power-play.
2. Knowledge engineering is primarily soft systems analysis. Discuss.
3. Derive at least one example of corporate knowledge at the operational, administrative and strategic levels of a business.
4. Take a conventional technical information system, such as an order-processing system, and analyse it as a system of signs.
5. Take any sign used in the system in 4. Break it up into the component elements of data, information, knowledge and subject.

REFERENCES

Anderson P.B. (1991). *A Theory of Computer Semiotics: Semiotic Approaches to the Construction and Assessment of Computer Systems*. Cambridge University Press, Cambridge.
Backhouse J., Liebenau J. and Land F. (1991). On the discipline of information systems. *Journal of Information Systems*, **1**(1), 19–27.

Checkland P. (1980). *Systems Thinking, Systems Practice*. John Wiley, Chichester.
Checkland P. and Scholes J. (1990). *Soft Systems Methodology in Action*. John Wiley, Chichester
Lai K-Y., Thomas W.M. and Yu K-C. (1988). Object lens: a 'spreadsheet' for cooperative work. *ACM Trans. on Office Information Systems*, **6**(4), 332–353.
Liebenau J. and Backhouse J. (1990). *Understanding Information: An Introduction*. Macmillan, Houndmills, Basingstoke.
Sowa J.F. (1984). *Conceptual Structures: Information Processing in Mind and Machine*. Addison-Wesley, Reading, MA.
Stamper R.K. (1973). *Information in Business and Administrative Systems*. Batsford, London.
Stamper R.K. (1985). Information: mystical fluid or a subject for scientific enquiry? *The Computer Journal*, **28**(3).
Tsitchizris D.C. and Lochovsky F.H. (1982). *Data Models*. Prentice-Hall, Englewood Cliffs, NJ.
Willcocks L. and Mason D. (1987). *Computerizing Work: People, Systems Design and Workplace Relations*. Paradigm, London.

KNOWLEDGE REPRESENTATION

3.1 INTRODUCTION

The term *knowledge representation* is conventionally used purely in the domain of AI. However, this is a narrow usage of the term. Most of what we mean by computing, particularly commercial computing, is knowledge representation. Knowledge representation is not simply the domain of the AI worker, it is of profound concern to the information systems professional.

This chapter is designed to support this thesis. Our main aim is to distinguish between the conventional senses of the terms data, information and knowledge and how these terms apply in commercial computing. This means discussing the idea of a data model, a semantic data model and a representation formalism. We conclude with a re-examination of the conventional definition of these terms and a reassessment of the knowledge engineering endeavour.

3.2 FACT BASES

Data are facts. Facts are relationships between real-world objects. Hence, we might relate Joe Bloggs to the project on which he is working – the accounts receivable project.

Facts are conventionally stored in databases. A database is a fact base, usually a large fact base. A database is an organized repository for facts. The overall purpose of such a system is to maintain data for some set of enterprise objectives. Normally, such objectives fall within the domain of administration. Most database systems are built to store the facts required for the running of the day-to-day activities of some organization.

A database conforms to some data model. The term data model is used to describe an architecture for data. Any data model is generally held to be made up of three components (Tsitchizris and Lochovsky, 1982):

1. A set of data structures.
2. A set of data operators.
3. A set of inherent integrity rules.

These three components are frequently referred to as data definition, data manipulation and data integrity respectively.

A distinction is frequently made between the intension of a database and the extension of a database. These terms, taken from formal logic, describe the following aspects of a database:

1. The intension of a database is a set of definitions which describe the structure of a given database; i.e. what data structures are used and what integrity constraints hold.
2. The extension of a database is the total set of all data in a database.

Both the intension and extension of a database must conform to the tenets of a given data model.

3.2.1 The relational data model

The most popular contemporary data model is the relational data model (Codd, 1970). The relational data model is intrinsically simple. There is only one data structure in it – the disciplined table or relation. The operators of the model all act on such tables to produce new tables. The operators are bundled together in a set known as the relational algebra. There are also only two inherent integrity rules in the relational data model. One is known as entity integrity, the other is called referential integrity.

A relation is a disciplined table which obeys a certain restricted set of rules:

1. Every relation in a database must have a distinct name.
2. Every column in a relation must have a distinct name within the relation.
3. All entries in a column must be of the same kind.
4. The ordering of columns in a relation is not significant.
5. Each row in a relation must be distinct. In other words, duplicate rows are not allowed in a relation.
6. The ordering of rows is not significant. There should be no implied order in the storage of rows in a relation.
7. Each cell or column/row intersection in a relation should contain only a so-called atomic value. In other words, multi-values are not allowed in a relation.

Two valid relations are given in Figs 3.1 and 3.2. One stores facts about employees of a building society (Fig. 3.1). The other stores facts about the society's branches (Fig. 3.2).

To enforce the property that duplicate rows are forbidden, each relation must have a so-called *primary key*. A primary key is one or more columns of a table whose values are

Employees

empno	ename	occupation	sex	DOB	salary	branchno
7369	Smith	Clerk	male	17-DEC-57	8000	10
7499	Allen	Advisor	female	20-FEB-62	16000	20
7521	Ward	Advisor	female	22-FEB-63	12500	10
7566	Jones	Manager	male	02-APR-70	29750	10
7654	Martin	Advisor	male	28-SEP-68	12500	10
7698	Blake	Manager	female	01-MAY-50	28500	20
7782	Clarke	Manager	male	09-JUN-49	24500	30
7788	Scott	Accountant	male	09-NOV-64	30000	10
7839	King	Director	female	17-NOV-62	50000	10
7844	Turner	Advisor	male	08-SEP-63	15000	30
7876	Adams	Clerk	male	23-SEP-60	11000	30
7900	James	Clerk	male	03-DEC-58	9500	20
7902	Ford	Accountant	male	02-DEC-59	30000	10
7934	Miller	Clerk	female	23-JAN-65	13000	20

Figure 3.1 A relation storing information about the society's employees.

Branches

branchno	bname	location
10	High St.	Cardiff
20	Manor Way	Swansea
30	Gabalfa	Cardiff
40	Mill St.	Pontypridd

Figure 3.2 A relation storing information about the society's branches.

used to uniquely identify each of the rows in a table. *Empno* is the primary key of *employees* and *branchno* is the primary key of *branches*.

The primary unit of data in the relational data model is the data item, for example, a part number, a customer number or a person's date of birth. Such data items are said to be non-decomposable or atomic. A set of such data items of the same type is said to be a *domain*. For example, the domain of employee numbers is the set of all possible employee numbers. Domains are therefore pools of values from which actual values appearing in the columns of a table are drawn.

Foreign keys are the glue of relational systems. They are the means of interconnecting the information stored in a series of disparate tables. A foreign key is a column or group of columns of some table which draws its values from the same domain as the primary key of some other table in the database. In our personnel example, *branchno* is a foreign key in the *employees* table. This column draws its values from the same domain as the *brancho* column – the primary key – of the *branches* table.

The relational algebra is a set of some eight operators. Each operator takes one or more relations as input and produces one relation as output. The three main operators of the algebra are *select*, *project* and *join*. Using these three operators most of the manipulation required of relational systems can be accomplished.

1. Select/Restrict. The *select* or *restrict* operator of the relational algebra takes a single relation as input and produces a single relation as output. Select is a 'horizontal slicer'. It extracts rows from the input relation matching a given condition and passes them to the output relation.
2. Project. The *project* operator takes a single relation as input and produces a single relation as output. *Project* is a 'vertical slicer'.
3. Join. The *join* operator takes two relations as input and produces one relation as output. A number of distinct types of *join* have been identified. Probably the most commonly used is the *natural join*, a development of the *equi-join*. The *equi-join* operator combines two tables together but only for records matching a given condition. Natural join is an equi-join followed by a project of one of the join columns.

Entity integrity concerns primary keys. Entity integrity is an integrity rule which states that every table must have a primary key and that the column or columns chosen to be the primary key should be unique and not null.

Referential integrity concerns foreign keys. The referential integrity rule states that any foreign key value can be in one of two states. The usual state of affairs is that the foreign key value refers to a primary key value of some table in the database. Occasionally, and this will depend on the rules of the organization, a foreign key value can be null. In this case we are explicitly saying that either there is no relationship between the objects represented in the database or that this relationship is unknown.

3.2.2 The database sub-language SQL

One of the major formalisms which define the present generation of relational database management products is Structured Query Language, or SQL for short. SQL was originally designed as a query language based on the relational algebra; however, it is a lot more than simply a query language – Codd refers to it as a database sub-language. This database sub-language is becoming the standard interface to relational and non-relational DBMS.

SQL comes in three major parts:

1. A data definition language (DDL) with integrity enhancement.
2. A data manipulation language (DML).
3. A data control language (DCL).

We give here a brief introduction to SQL, the aim being merely to illustrate the possibilities of the language. More detail is given in Beynon-Davies (1991b).

The structure for tables in a database can be set up using the *create table* command. For example:

```
CREATE TABLE<table name>
(<attribute name> <data type> (<length)>,
..        ..   ..;
..        ..   ..)
```

```
CREATE TABLE branches
(branchno char(4),
bname char(15),
location char(15))
```

The *create table* command allows us to specify a name for a table, and the names, data types and lengths of each of the attributes in the table. Many contemporary implementations of SQL have no direct mechanism for enforcing the notion of primary and foreign keys. An addendum to the ANSI standard, however, specifies a primary and foreign key clause:

```
CREATE TABLE<table name>
(<attribute name> <data type> (<length)>,
..        ..   ..,
..        ..   ..)
PRIMARY KEY (<attribute name>)
FOREIGN KEY (<attribute name> IDENTIFIES <table name>)
```

```
CREATE TABLE employees
(empno char(4),
ename char(20),
occupation char(20),
sex char(10)
dob date,
branchno char(4))
PRIMARY KEY (empno)
FOREIGN KEY (branchno IDENTIFIES branches)
```

Referential integrity also involves specifying precisely what should happen in related tables when updates and deletes occur in a target table. The specifications below restrict the deletion of a branch record until all matching employee records have been deleted. They also specify that any change made to the branch number of a branch record should be reflected in all relevant employee records.

```
CREATE TABLE employees
(empno char(4),
ename char(20),
occupation char(20)
sex char(10)
dob date,
branchno char(4))
PRIMARY KEY (empno)
FOREIGN KEY (branchno IDENTIFIES branches)
DELETE OF branchno RESTRICTED,
UPDATE OF branchno CASCADES)
```

Having created a structure for the tables in our database, we can enter data into such tables using the *insert* command:

```
INSERT INTO <table name>
(<attribute1>, <attribute2>,...)
VALUES
('<value1>','<value2>',...)

INSERT INTO branches
(branchno,bname,location)
VALUES
(06,'Whitchurch Rd','Whitchurch')
```

We also maintain the ongoing data in the database through use of the *update* and *delete* commands:

```
UPDATE <table name>
SET <attribute1>  =  <new value>
<attribute2>  =  <new value>
...
WHERE <condition>

UPDATE employees

SET salary  =  salary  +  (salary *0.1)
WHERE empno  =  '7782'

DELETE FROM <table name>
WHERE <condition>

DELETE FROM employees
WHERE empno  =  '7875'
```

Although SQL has a data definition and file maintenance subset, the language was designed primarily as a means for extracting data from a database. Such extraction is accomplished through use of the *select* command: a combination of the *restrict*, *project*, and *join* operators of the relational algebra.

Retrieval is accomplished by a combination of the *select*, *from* and *where* clauses:

```
SELECT <attribute1 name>, <attribute2 name>,...
FROM <table name>
WHERE <condition>

SELECT empno, ename, occupation
FROM employees
WHERE job  =  'Clerk'
```

SQL performs relational joins by indicating common attributes in the where clause of a *select* statement. For instance, the *select* statement below extracts data of relevance to clerks from the branches and employees tables, and orders it by salary.

```
SELECT empno, ename, salary, bname, location
FROM employees, branches
```

```
WHERE employees.branchno  =  branches.branchno
AND occupation  =  'Clerk'
ORDER BY salary
```

The primary mechanism for enforcing control issues in SQL is through the concept of a view. Views are virtual tables which act as 'windows' on the database of real tables. The view below establishes a virtual table for use by managers of branches in Cardiff. Such managers granted access only to this view would be unable to see information of relevance to other branches in the company.

```
CREATE VIEW cardiff__branches
AS SELECT empno, ename, salary, bname
FROM employees, branches
WHERE employees.branchno  =  branches.branchno
AND location  =  'Cardiff'
ORDER BY occupation
```

3.3 INFORMATION BASES

Information is meaningful data – interpreted facts. Most contemporary database systems only form part of a larger information system. The information system forms a layer of interpretation around facts stored in the database.

The main problem with classic data models like the relational data model is that they still maintain a fundamental record-orientation (King and McCleod, 1985). In other words, the meaning of the information in the database – its semantics – is not readily apparent from the database itself. Semantic information must be consciously applied by the user of databases using the classic approach. For this reason, a number of so-called semantic data models have been proposed. Semantic data models attempt to provide a more expressive means of representing the meaning of information than is available in the classic models.

Probably the most frequently cited of the semantic data models is the entity–relationship data model (E–R model). In the E–R model the real world is represented in terms of entities, the relationships between entities and the attributes associated with entities. Entities represent objects of interest in the real world such as *employees*, *departments* and *projects*. Relationships represent named associations between entities. A department *employs* many employees. An employee *is assigned to* a number of projects. *Employs* and *is assigned to* are both relationships in the entity–relationship approach. Attributes are properties of an entity or relationship. *Name* is an attribute of the *employee* entity. *Duration of employment* is an attribute of the *employs* relationship.

The original entity–relationship model has been extended in a number of ways (Teorey *et al.*, 1986). One of the most important extensions is the support for generalization hierarchies (Smith and Smith, 1977). This allows us to declare certain entities as instances of other entities. For instance, *manager*, *secretary* and *technician* might all be declared instances of an *employee* entity. Likewise, *sales managers*, *production managers*, etc. would all be declared instances of the *manager* entity. The important consequence of this facility is that entities lower down in the generalization hierarchy inherit the attributes of entities higher up in the hierarchy. Hence, a *sales manager* would inherit properties of managers in general, and indeed of employees in general.

3.4 KNOWLEDGE BASES

In the field of expert systems, knowledge representation implies some systematic means of encoding what an expert knows about a knowledge domain in an appropriate medium. At a very general level it involves mapping knowledge at the psychological level into a representation of knowledge at the computational level.

Patrick Henry Winston has defined a representation as being, 'a set of syntactic and semantic conventions that make it possible to describe things' (Winston, 1984). The syntax of a representation specifies a set of rules for combining symbols and arrangements of symbols to form statements in the representation formalism. The semantics of a representation specify how such statements should be interpreted. That is, how can we derive meaning from them?

Three main formalisms for representing knowledge have found favour in knowledge engineering (Nilsson, 1982):

1. Production rules.
2. Structured objects.
3. Predicate logic.

In this section we introduce an architecture based on a hybrid of production rules and structured objects. This type of architecture is becoming increasingly popular in many commercial expert system shells.

Production rules consist of condition and action pairs of the form:

IF <condition>
AND <condition>
AND ...
THEN <action>
AND <action>
AND ...

Conditions and actions are usually made up of associations between objects and values. In the syntax of most shells it is usual to see a condition or action expressed in the form:

<object> is <value>

as in:

employmentStatus is selfEmployed

The keyword *is* or *are* is used to delimit the object from the value. A rule incorporating this condition might be:

IF employmentStatus is selfEmployed
AND jobType is manual
THEN application is unlikely

which is to be read as, 'if a person's employment status is self employed and the person is employed in a manual occupation, then that person is unlikely to make a pension application'.

Each object in a series of production rules can be described by a frame (Minsky, 1975). A frame is a packet of knowledge which provides a description of an object. Each frame is made up of a series of slots. Each slot may be assigned a number of different fillers.

For the purposes of our discussion we shall assume that each object is characterized by the following generic slots:

Name:
Description:
Type:
Values:
Default:

The *name* slot acts as the identifier for the object. The *type* slot defines the data type of the object – numeric, text, list. The *description* slot acts as a reference for documentation purposes. The *values* slot determines the allowed values for the object. The *default* slot indicates the value to be taken by the object in the face of uncertainty on behalf of the user.

The objects involved in the rule above might therefore be defined as follows:

Name: employmentStatus
Description: the employment status associated with a customer
Type: text
Values: employed, selfEmployed
Default: employed

Name: jobType
Description: the main occupational group of the customer
Type: text
Values: manual, nonManual
Default: nonManual

Name: application
Description: the likelihood of a customer making a pension application
Type: text
Values: likely, unlikely
Default: unlikely

An expert system designed using the production rule formalism is said to be a production system. A production system consists of a rule base, a rule interpreter which decides how and when to apply the rules, and a working memory that holds data, goals or intermediate results.

The most basic function of working memory is to hold facts. A fact is a relationship between an object and a value. These facts are used by the interpreter to drive rules in the sense that the presence of these elements in working memory trigger some rules in the rule base by satisfying their conditions. For instance, suppose we have the following two elements in our working memory:

employmentStatus: selfEmployed
jobType: manual

These two facts satisfy the conditions in the rule above, since both the objects and values match against the conditions of the rule.

The usual situation, however, is one in which the working memory contains many facts. Only some combination of these facts will give rise to assignments which satisfy the conditions of some rule. Other assignments of facts to rules will be unsuccessful. This means that the rule interpreter must have some means of 'backtracking' – that is, undoing an unproductive move and exploring alternatives.

The rule interpreter for a rule base can therefore be described in terms of a cycle of actions:

1. Match rules against facts in working memory.
2. If more than one rule can be matched with the existing facts, decide which one should be used.
3. Apply the rule. This might mean adding a new fact to working memory or deleting an old one. Then go to step 1.

The inference described above is a forward-chaining or data-directed inference mechanism. In this type of mechanism, inference moves forward from data stored in working memory to the goal to be solved. The system does this by attempting to match the facts stored in working memory against the conditions or IF parts of the rules in the rule base.

Many expert systems employ an alternative type of inference strategy known as backward chaining. In a backward-chaining system, the user first selects a goal for the system to solve. The system attempts to solve this goal by searching through the knowledge base for a rule which has a structure in its conclusion, or THEN part, which matches the structure of the goal. Backward chaining is hence often referred to as goal-directed chaining.

3.5 A BLURRING OF TERMS

The term 'knowledge engineering' has become inextricably linked with the development of expert systems, particularly with systems built using the formalism of production rules. This is a limited definition. It does not fully encompass what we might reasonably expect from a computational definition of knowledge.

In Chapter 1 we used Winston's definition of knowledge: *the symbolic representation of some named universe of discourse.* Symbolic representation generally means organizing representations of real-world objects together in three component structures:

1. Facts
2. Rules
3. Inference

Facts are relationships between real-world objects. Hence:

1. Mr Lee's age is 43 years
2. Mr Lee holds account 4234
3. Mr Lee is a building society customer
4. Account 4234 is an ordinary-share building society account
5. Ordinary-share building society accounts are a safe investment
6. Customers are a kind of person

are all facts in that they relate real-world objects. Facts 1 and 2, however, are subtly different from facts 3 and 4, which are in turn different in type from facts 5 and 6.

Facts 1 and 2 relate objects to attributes and values – Mr Lee to his actual age, and Mr Lee to the account he holds. Facts 3 and 4 relate objects to object classes. Fact 3 defines Mr Lee (object) as an instance of the class of customers. Fact 4 defines account 4234 as an instance of the class of ordinary-share building society accounts. Facts 5 and 6 relate object classes together. Fact 5 declares ordinary-share building society accounts to be a kind of, a subclass of, investment. Fact 6 declares customers to be a subclass of the class of persons.

Facts 1 and 2 are the classic stuff of which conventional databases, such as relational databases, are made. Facts 3 to 6 are engaging the area of interpretation – the assignment of meaning. We are moving here from a consideration of the extension of databases to the intension of databases. It is to the storage of these kinds of relationships that the development of semantic data models has been directed.

Rules are mechanisms for generating new facts from existing facts. We generate new facts from existing facts via a process of inference. Inference determines in what way we assign facts to rules to generate new facts. Hence:

1. Middle-age is 35 to 50
2. Middle-aged customers are cautious
3. Cautious customers prefer safe investments

are all rules. We might use these rules, with the facts previously established, in the following process of inference:

1. We apply fact 1 to rule 1 to give us the fact: (fact 7) Mr Lee is middle-aged
2. We apply fact 7 to rule 2 to generate the fact: (fact 8) Mr Lee is cautious
3. We apply fact 8 and fact 3 to rule 3 to generate the new inference: Mr Lee prefers safe investments.

Most of the inference process described above adheres to the principle of forward chaining as explained in Section 3.4. Note, however, there is at least one hidden inference in the process above. We have assumed that the relationship documented in fact 3 allows us to substitute Mr Lee for customer. This is actually a specialization rule.

The distinction between facts, rules and inference is therefore a hazy one. Facts 3 to 6, for instance, actually have inference rules associated with them. This is because facts 3 and 4 represent ISA (Is-Instance-Of) relationships while facts 5 and 6 represent AKO (A-Kind-Of) relationships. Both ISA and AKO relationships are popular mechanisms of abstraction (Smith and Smith, 1977).

The major form of inference associated with ISA and AKO relationships is referred to as inheritance. Inheritance is the process by which lower-level objects in a generalization hierarchy are characterized by properties defined in higher levels of the hierarchy. Describing an ordinary-share building society account to be a type of investment, for instance, means that ordinary-share accounts inherit the properties of investments in general.

Knowledge and its representation is probably the central issue in computing. In conventional knowledge representation, the facts, rules and inference relevant to some application are all intertwined in programs and tightly-coupled files. Database systems have enabled the separation of large bodies of facts from the rules and inference embodied in application programs. Expert systems have encouraged the separation of rules from inference mechanisms. The aim of a true knowledge base management system will be to enforce a clean separation between facts, rules and inference.

3.6 CONCLUSION

In much the same vein as that taken by Mylopoulos *et al.* (1990), this chapter is 'based on the premise that information systems development is knowledge intensive and that the primary responsibility of any language intended to support this task is to be able to formally represent the relevant knowledge'.

Although we have defined knowledge engineering as the discipline devoted to the building of knowledge base systems, our definition of a knowledge base system is a larger one than simply the set of rules in some production system. This gives knowledge engineering a larger role to play than merely the development of standalone expert systems. As we shall see in the chapter that follows, the current generation of expert system shells are expanding into the database area, while the current generation of database systems are exploiting the capabilities of expert systems. What is likely to happen in the relatively near future is that knowledge representation languages and environments will be the primary means for building information systems.

3.7 RECALL EXERCISES

1. Define what is meant by a data model.
2. In what way can we say that a relational database is an example of knowledge representation?
3. What is meant by a semantic data model?
4. What is a production rule?
5. Produce a set of production rules to represent the rules in Section 3.5.
6. What is a frame?
7. Produce a set of frames for the objects in Section 3.5.

8. Distinguish between forward and backward chaining. Illustrate these mechanisms in terms of the rules built in 5.
9. Distinguish between facts, information and rules.
10. What is inference?
11. In what way is the statement, *Jones has a salary of £15 000 p.a.*, qualitatively different from the statement, *Jones is an employee*?
12. What is inheritance?

3.8 OPEN-ENDED EXERCISES

1. Another abstraction mechanism much discussed in both AI and database work is the PARTOF relation. PARTOF is used to define an object as an aggregation or assembly of other objects. Identify a set of PARTOF relations appropriate to the finance sector.
2. In what ways are relations like AKO and ISA intensional relations?
3. In what way do AKO and ISA relations impinge on the problem of data integrity?
4. All representation is abstraction. We necessarily lose something in the process of representing it. Discuss.
5. Why is information systems development knowledge-intensive?

REFERENCES

Beynon-Davies P. (1991b). *Relational Database Systems: A Pragmatic Approach*. Blackwell Scientific, Oxford.

Codd E.F. (1970). A relational model for large shared data banks. *Comm.ACM* **13** (6).

King R. and McCleod D. (1985). Semantic data models. In S.Bing Yao (ed.) *Principles of Database Design. Vol 1: Logical Organizations*. Prentice-Hall, Englewood Cliffs, NJ.

Minsky M. (1975). A framework for representing knowledge. In P.H.Winston (ed.). *The Psychology of Computer Vision*. McGraw-Hill, New York.

Mylopoulos J., Borgida A., Jarke M. and Koubarakis M. (1990). Telos: representing knowledge about information systems. *ACM Trans. on Information Systems* **8**(4), 325–362.

Nilsson N.J. (1982). *Principles of Artificial Intelligence*. Tioga, Palo Alto, CA.

Smith J.M. and Smith D.C.P. (1977). Database abstractions: aggregation and generalization. *ACM Trans. on Database Systems* **2**(2), 105–133.

Teorey T.J., Yang D. and Fry J.P. (1986). A logical design methodology for relational databases using the extended entity–relationship model. *ACM Computing Surveys* **18**, 197–222.

Winston P.H. (1984). *Artificial Intelligence*. Addison-Wesley, Reading, MA.

4

EXPERT SYSTEMS, EXPERT SYSTEM SHELLS AND EXPERT DATABASE SYSTEMS

4.1 INTRODUCTION

In the previous chapter we discussed the issue of knowledge representation both in conventional information systems work and in the field of AI. Knowledge representation in conventional information systems work primarily involves data modelling, particularly semantic data modelling. Knowledge representation in AI primarily involves choosing an appropriate formalism, of which production rules and structured objects are certainly the most prevalent. In this chapter we aim to cement the discussion by discussing the pragmatic implementation of knowledge representation both in the database and AI world. In the database world this means discussing SQL and proposed semantic extensions to database sub-languages of this type. In the world of AI it means discussing the architecture of a typical expert system shell.

The chapter is therefore divided into two parts. In the first part we begin by identifying what is meant by the term *expert system*, and what sort of problems expert systems are designed for. We then consider the distinction between an expert system and an expert system shell, and detail some of the advantages of using shells for expert system development. The section concludes by considering the place of the micro- and mainframe-based expert system shells in knowledge engineering.

In the second part we consider the issue of database integrity and how a number of extensions to database sub-languages like SQL will gradually converge with the knowledge representation formalisms of expert system shells.

Our aim is to demonstrate how the knowledge engineers of the future will not simply be the engineers of expert systems. They will need to be the engineers of databases and information bases as well.

4.2 EXPERT SYSTEMS

There are at least three ways of defining an expert system:

1. Intensionally, particularly in terms of some idea of objectives or function.
2. Extensionally, in terms of major areas of application.
3. Architecturally, in terms of major components.

We shall give a brief intensional and extensional definition of the term expert system in this section. An architectural definition is given in the next section.

4.2.1 Objectives

There are many definitions of the term expert system available. Below, we list some of the most popular:

> A computer system that achieves high levels of performance in task areas that, for human beings, require years of special education and training. (Hayes-Roth *et al.*, 1983).

> A computer program using expert knowledge to attain high levels of performance in a narrow problem area. (Waterman, 1986).

> An expert system is a computer system that encapsulates specialist knowledge about a particular domain of expertise and is capable of making intelligent decisions within that domain. (Forsyth, 1989).

> An expert system is a computer system that uses a representation of human expertise in a particular domain in order to perform functions similar to those normally performed by a human expert in that domain. (Goodall, 1985).

> An expert system is a computer system that encapsulates specialist knowledge about a particular domain of expertise and is capable of making intelligent decisions within that domain. (Jackson, 1990).

The common elements of these definitions are that:

1. An expert system is a computer system.
2. It is designed to emulate some aspects of human expertise.

But what is expertise? Johnson usefully defines an expert as being:

> . . . a person who, because of training and experience, is able to do things the rest of us cannot; experts are not only proficient but also smooth and efficient in the actions they take. Experts know a great many things and have tricks and caveats for applying what they know to problems and tasks; they are also good at ploughing through irrelevant information in order to get at basic issues, and they are good at recognising the problems they face as instances of types with which they are familiar. (Johnson, 1983).

4.2.2 Application

Another way of defining the term expert system is extensionally in terms of contemporary usage. Most contemporary expert system applications fall into a few distinct types (Hayes-Roth *et al.*, 1983):

1. Interpretation systems that infer descriptions from observables. For example, surveillance systems, speech understanding, image analysis, chemical structure elucidation.
2. Prediction systems that infer likely consequences from given situations. For instance, weather forecasting, demographic prediction, traffic prediction, military forecasting.
3. Diagnosis systems that infer system malfunctions from observables. For example, medical, mechanical and software diagnosis.
4. Design systems that develop configurations of objects that satisfy the constraints of a design problem. For instance, digital circuit layout and building design.
5. Planning systems that design actions. For example, automatic programming, robot movement, military strategy.
6. Monitoring systems that compare observations of system behaviour to features that seem crucial to successful plan outcomes. For instance, power plan monitoring, air traffic control.
7. Debugging systems that prescribe remedies for malfunctions. For example, program debugging.
8. Repair systems that develop and execute plans to administer a remedy for some diagnosed problem. For instance, automotive, avionic or computer maintenance.
9. Instruction systems that diagnose and debug student behaviour. For instance, the whole area of adaptive computer-aided instruction.
10. Control systems that adaptively govern the overall control of the system. For instance, battle and business management.

4.3 EXPERT SYSTEM SHELLS

The vast majority of the early expert systems (e.g. MYCIN) were built using a traditional AI language such as LISP. The knowledge in such a system was therefore 'hard-wired'.

As knowledge engineering developed as a discipline, it became evident that new expert systems need not be built from scratch each time using languages like LISP, but that they could borrow a great deal from previously built systems. The way to do this was to separate out the knowledge specific to the particular domain from that part which drives the expert system. The former entity is now usually referred to as the knowledge base, while the latter is called an inference engine.

This strategy resulted in a new category of knowledge engineering tool – the *expert system shell*. A shell is an expert system without the domain-specific knowledge.

4.3.1 Architecture of an expert system shell

An expert system shell is a tool for building expert systems. Fig. 4.1 illustrates the architecture of a generic expert system shell. The shell is made up of a number of components:

1. The knowledge base. The repository of facts and rules that represent the domain-specific knowledge.
2. The inference engine. The driver of the system in the sense of making inferences from the knowledge base.

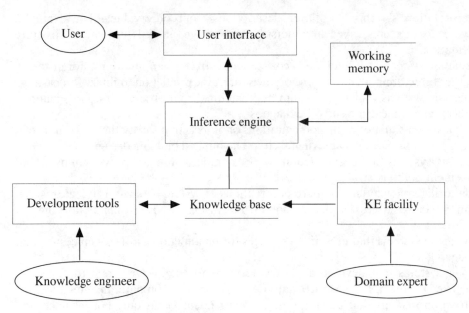

Figure 4.1 Architecture of a generic expert system shell.

3. The working memory. A data area for storing intermediate results generated by problem-solving.
4. Development tools. Designed for use by knowledge engineers, these are tools for building and testing the knowledge base.
5. User interface. Allows end-users to run the expert system and interact with it. One of the most important interactions is with the system's explanation facility. This enables the user to ask questions of the system, about how, for instance, the system came to a particular conclusion.
6. Knowledge acquisition facility. This is a set of facilities designed primarily to enable a domain expert to impart his expertise to the system directly, i.e. without the intervention of a knowledge engineer. This topic will be discussed more fully in the subsequent chapter on knowledge elicitation.

If we make the analogy with conventional software, AI languages like LISP and PROLOG are really third generation languages for knowledge base work comparable with COBOL and Pascal in conventional information processing. Expert system shells are higher-level languages or fourth-generation languages for knowledge engineering comparable with conventional tools such as FOCUS.

Appendices 1 and 2 introduce two commonly available expert system shells.

4.3.2 Advantages of expert system shells

One of the most difficult phases of expert system development is the construction of the first prototype system. Shells allow developers to rapidly prototype a solution to a problem. As such, they have a clear part to play in the rapid prototyping approach to knowledge engineering which we shall discuss in Chapter 5.

An expert system developed in a language such as LISP can be said to be relatively unstructured, in the sense that LISP does not impose many constraints on the finalized system. LISP is a general programming language, and as such permits flexibility. It may also, however, be seen as a disadvantage in the sense that it forces developers to resolve problems of detailed structure prior to doing any substantive work. In contrast, shells impose prior structure thus enabling developers to concentrate on substantive content rather than form.

A major reason that expert systems are still a developing technology is that there are not enough skilled knowledge engineers to go around. Shells help to reduce the levels of skill required by developers in effectively supplying some of the required expertise. Thus shells can be a major influence in alleviating the expert system development bottleneck.

4.3.3 Shells on PCs

Early shells such as EMYCIN (a development of the MYCIN project) (Van Melle *et al.*, 1981) ran on mainframe or mini-computers. Recently however a number of expert system shells have become available for the personal computer market. The primary motivations for implementing an expert system on a micro-computer are low cost, availability and transportability (Schafer, 1985).

Low cost and availability make it possible to distribute cost-effectively multiple copies of the same system around an organization or between organizations. As regards transportability, the small size and robust design of PCs make them appropriate for applications where physical space is limited and/or harsh environments may be encountered – e.g. the North Sea.

These factors influence what is perhaps the primary advantage of implementing expert systems on PCs, namely that they are ideal tools for experimentation, exploration, learning and assessment. It is possible for a company to experiment with expert systems without making a sizeable investment in resources. As a result, it affords companies a low risk opportunity for determining the potential of this new area for their applications work.

The software house Logica, for instance, has used PC-based shells to first investigate the feasibility of a particular expert systems application. Being sure of its feasibility, it then often chooses to develop the full system in a traditional procedural language such as C to improve performance and the ability to interface with other more conventional software (Maney and Reid, 1986).

4.3.3 Disadvantages of PC-based expert systems

Many expert system professionals are extremely sceptical about the application of PCs to realistic knowledge engineering. Such scepticism seems to centre mainly around hardware issues: the lack of memory, lack of processing speed, and lack of adequate secondary storage of PCs. This group of knowledge engineers generally look to specialist workstations for expert system development. All of these factors are, of course, subject to technological progress. In terms of hardware, there is a blurring, for instance, at the present time between what we mean by the terms micro-computer, mini-computer, and mainframe. In terms of software, more and more shells originally developed for the PC market are offering mini- and mainframe versions.

The present shells, particularly the PC-based variety, have however tended traditionally to restrict themselves to only one main form of reasoning – usually backward chaining. This means that if this style of reasoning does not suit your application, then neither will the shell. In a similar manner, a shell normally implements only one form of knowledge representation; the most popular seems to be the production rule approach. Many shells do not implement other representations such as structured objects, and many do not offer any way of working with uncertain or incomplete knowledge. This is often a setback in implementing any realistic expert system.

4.3.4 Expert systems on mainframes

Popolizio and Capelli (1989) estimate that of approximately 2200 commercial expert systems applications in North America almost half were developed and approximately 60 per cent delivered on IBM PCs or PC-compatibles. Most of the remaining 40 per cent were on specialist LISP workstations. The predominance of the PC as the platform of choice for commercial expert system development is largely the result of a change which took place in the organization of data processing departments in the 1980s.

It is no accident that the acceptance of PC-based systems coincides with the heyday of the information centre. The ability of expert systems to provide more 'intelligent', automated decision support means that such systems exerted their initial appeal on middle management in the front-line of business activities.

There are a number of forces at work, however, that are likely to dislodge the PC from its pre-eminent position in the world of commercial expert systems. The preservation and distribution of corporate knowledge is probably one of the most important goals of most commercial organizations. Since the mainframe is the usual repository for much of that corporate knowledge it seems natural to envisage the rise of mainframe-based expert systems over the next few years.

Three areas of application seem currently to be receiving the most attention:

1. Automated help desks. This is a group of applications that provide information about the initiation or circumvention of interruptions to routine computer-related tasks performed by the end-user.
2. Performance analysis. Monitoring the performance of large multi-user systems is heavily knowledge-intensive. Operators and analysts have concocted many heuristics for the effective running of such systems. The use of knowledge base systems to capture and disseminate such heuristics can mean the difference between the smooth-running and complete failure of many systems.
3. Automated operators. One of the most attainable applications is the reduction and control of messages to an operator's terminal. Knowledge base systems can be used to analyse and filter critical messages from the routine.

Most mainframe shells sacrifice the attractive user interfaces provided by PC shells for two major advantages. First, they allow developers to draw data directly from a variety of databases run under a number of DBMS. Second, many have the ability to reside within, and invoke the resources of, a transaction processing system such as CICS.

4.4 MULTIPLE PLATFORMS

Despite many disadvantages, PC-based expert system shells are here to stay. The major factor is probably PC users' growing awareness of knowledge engineering in particular, and AI in general. Expert systems on personal computers provide an excellent medium for getting an immediate feel for the knowledge engineering discipline. As such, they provide a productive vehicle for the initial training of the new generation of knowledge engineers needed by Britain, and the rest of the world.

In addition to serving as platforms for prototyping, and for small applications, it is likely that many PC-based expert systems will cooperate in a symbiotic way with their mainframe cousins. This allows the power inherent in the corporate knowledge resident on the mainframe to be coupled with the sophisticated interface available on the PC.

4.5 EXPERT DATABASE SYSTEMS

Expert systems research started several years ago with a number of notable academic successes. In recent times, the area has been characterized by a heavy emphasis on commercialization. An expert system is based on two fundamental principles: the appropriate representation of domain knowledge, and the control of this domain knowledge.

Database management systems (DBMS) research has some notable practical successes, particularly in the operational area of database systems. Data models that have been developed for databases share the same overall objectives as knowledge representation schemes for expert systems; that is, to represent some 'slice of reality' (see Chapter 3).

Clearly, the combination of the two technologies would benefit both expert and database systems. Expert systems, and AI technology in general, will contribute to database systems in areas such as providing a useful reasoning ability in query optimization tasks. DBMS technology will contribute to expert systems in giving them the ability to access large collections of facts and also to apply features such as concurrency control, data security and optimized access to knowledge base items.

There are, however, a number of ways in which these technologies can be combined. For the purposes of discussion we shall roughly distinguish between four types of *expert database systems*, or EDS for short (Al-Zobaidie and Grimson, 1987)

1. An enhanced database system.
2. An enhanced expert system.
3. An interdependent expert system and database.
4. A higher-order synthesis – a knowledge base management system (KBMS).

The first two types are examples of what we might call an evolutionary approach to building EDS (Mylopoulos, 1989). This approach treats databases and/or expert systems as starting points and move in an evolutionary fashion towards the goal of a knowledge base management system (KBMS).

Many other people believe, however, that melding expert systems technology with database technology through some sort of fusion is unlikely to result in a happy union.

One group maintains that it is far better to employ the known strengths of each tool and allow them to communicate down a common data channel to solve the sort of 'intelligent' tasks required of the new applications. This is the third type of EDS architecture – an interdependent expert system and database.

Yet another group prefers an alternative, revolutionary, approach to expert database systems. They wish to provide a higher-order synthesis by building a true KBMS. We must begin, they say, with a framework for knowledge representation to be supported by a KBMS and then develop a theory of KBMSs based on the features of this framework. They point to the relational data model as an example of the success of this approach. Codd originally proposed a theoretical data model which had to wait a number of years for practical fruition as a relational database management system. In the short term, this approach is unlikely to be productive if only because of the difficulties involved in demonstrating the computational tractability of such schemes. In the long term, however, this approach is probably the correct one given the likely advances in hardware and software.

4.5.1 A sample enhanced database system

A detailed discussion of expert database systems is given in Beynon-Davies (1991). In this section we discuss one type of expert database system known as an enhanced database system. In particular, we base our discussion on the work of the POSTGRES project.

The POSTGRES project at the University of Berkeley, California is a successor to the INGRES project, one of the first developed relational database management systems. Its overall aim is to develop a KBMS by straightforward and natural extensions to the INGRES relational database management system. The most important aspect of this work is POSTQUEL, an extension to the QUEL relational query language incorporating rule-like mechanisms (Stonebraker and Rowe, 1987). In this section we adapt the constructs slightly to make them work within an SQL environment.

Any SQL command can be turned into a rule by prefixing it with the keyword *always*. For instance, the following command in SQL raises the salary of all non-managerial employees if the system date (SYSDAT) equals their incremental date.

```
UPDATE employees
SET salary = salary *0.1
WHERE sysdat = increment_date
AND job<>'Manager'
```

To turn this command into a more general rule, however, we prefix the command with the term *always*:

```
ALWAYS UPDATE employees
SET salary = salary *0.1
WHERE sysdat = increment_date
AND job<>'Manager'
```

The command now appears, theoretically at least, to be continuously running. In practice, this rule will be implemented in one of two ways: either by early evaluation or by late evaluation.

Using early evaluation, the DBMS will awaken this command at the time that the system date is set to the incremental date. Hence, the command is awakened whenever a data-item that it needs is modified. Using late evaluation, the DBMS waits until somebody requests the salary of a given employee.

Collections of rules can interact. For example, suppose we have a second rule which checks that the salary of all managers is greater than the maximum earning non-management employee.

```
ALWAYS UPDATE employees
SET salary  =  salary *0.1
WHERE job  =  'Manager'
AND salary <  =
(SELECT MAX (salary)
FROM employees
WHERE job<>'Manager')
```

If both rules are evaluated by using early evaluation, then a forward-chaining control flow results. When a non-manager gets a new salary via the firing of the first rule, this may be propagated to a manager or managers via the firing of the second rule. On the other hand, late evaluation corresponds to backward chaining. A request for a manager's salary may cause a request for a non-manager's salary.

4.5.2 Database integrity

The classic application for AI technology within database systems is as mechanisms for ensuring database integrity. Database integrity is the problem of ensuring that a database contains only valid data; in other words, that it remains an accurate reflection of the real world it is attempting to model.

The conventional way of implementing integrity in information systems is via large amounts of procedural application code. However, an increasing number of people have discussed the desirability of placing integrity mechanisms within the remit of the database management system (DBMS). The DBMS in this conception should constitute a centralized resource for managing not only business data, but also business rules.

In such systems, the nature of our original definition of expertise, and indeed expert systems, changes subtly. Expertise is now less likely to be the prerogative of one individual or a limited group of individuals. It is also less likely to represent high-level, specialist knowledge. The stuff of expert database systems is now more likely to represent lower-level, corporate-wide knowledge.

4.6 CONCLUSION

Knowledge engineering is conventionally identified solely with expert systems and expert system shells. A brief definition of these terms from three different viewpoints has been provided in this chapter.

However, knowledge engineering is beginning to impact on one of the central struts of information systems work – database systems. It is likely that most information systems of the future will have some form of expert system component. This might be via a separate expert system running on a PC which accesses data on the corporate database. It is equally as likely, however, that the expert system will be an intrinsic part of the database system itself.

4.7 RECALL EXERCISES

1. What is the primary objective of an expert system?
2. What is meant by expertise?
3. List three application areas for expert systems.
4. Distinguish between an expert system and an expert system shell.
5. What is meant by the term 'expert database system'.
6. Discuss some of the advantages and disadvantages of expert systems on PCs.
7. Why is there likely to be a push to develop expert systems on mainframes?
8. What is database integrity and how are expert systems applicable?
9. In what way do enhanced database systems change the conventional conception of expertise and expert systems?

4.8 OPEN-ENDED EXERCISES

1. Dreyfus and Dreyfus (1986) have criticized the idea that expertise can be regarded as equivalent to rational calculation. They cast expertise as skilful performance in some domain; as a phenomenon not amenable to formal representation – *when things are proceeding normally, experts don't solve problems and don't make decisions; they do what normally works*. Discuss the consequences of this statement for expert systems work.
2. Of the application areas discussed in Section 4.2, which do you think are the most amenable to expert systems application?
3. The push has been to distribute more and more computing power throughout an organization. Some people see the day of the large, centralized mainframe to be limited. Discuss the consequences of this trend for expert systems development.

REFERENCES

Al-Zobaidie A. and Grimson J.B. (1987). Expert systems and database systems: how can they serve each other? *Expert Systems* **4**(1).
Beynon-Davies P. (1991). *Expert Database Systems: A Gentle Introduction*. McGraw-Hill, London.
Dreyfus H.L. and Dreyfus S.E. (1986). *Mind Over Machine: The Power of Human Intuition and Expertise in the Era of the Computer*. Basil Blackwell, Oxford.
Forsyth R. (Ed.) (1989). *Expert Systems: Principles and Case Studies*. 2nd Edn. Chapman and Hall, London.
Goodall A. (1985). *The Guide to Expert Systems*. Learned Information, Cambridge.
Hayes-Roth F., Waterman D. and Lenat D.B. (Eds.) (1983). *Building Expert Systems*. Addison-Wesley, Reading, MA.
Jackson P. (1990). *An Introduction to Expert Systems*. 2nd Edn. Addison-Wesley, Reading, MA.

Johnson P.E. (1983). What kind of expert system should a system be? *Journal of Medicine and Philosophy* **8**, 77–97.

Maney T. and Reid I. (1986) *A Management Guide to Artificial Intelligence*. Paradigm, London.

Mylopoulos J. (1989). On knowledge base management systems. In Mylopoulos J. and Brodie M. *Readings in AI and Database Systems*. Morgan Kauffmann, New York.

Popolizio J.J. and Capelli W.S. (1989). New shells for old iron. *Datamation*, April, 41–48.

Stonebraker M. and Rowe L.A. (1987). *The Design of Postgres*. Memorandum, Electronics Research Laboratory, University of California, Berkeley.

Waterman D.A. (1986). *A Guide to Expert Systems*. Addison-Wesley, Reading, MA.

Van Melle W., Shortliffe E.H., Buchanan B.G. (1981). EMYCIN: a domain independent system that aids in constructing knowledge based consultation programs. *Machine Intelligence*, Infotech State of the Art Report 9.

5

METHODS FOR KNOWLEDGE BASE SYSTEMS

5.1 INTRODUCTION

Knowledge base systems have come of age in the sense of being increasingly exploited in the commercial world. A number of questions remain, however. How are such systems built? How should they be built? How can knowledge base systems be integrated into conventional information systems?

This chapter begins the process of answering these questions. It presents first a description of a much-cited methodology for building expert systems. It then uses this as a basis for discussing the relationship between knowledge base system development and traditional software development. It makes the point that important work needs to be done in identifying what software and information engineering methodologies have to offer knowledge engineering and vice versa.

We illustrate the discussion by discussing an integrated proposal for a knowledge base systems development methodology – KADS.

5.2 THE FIVE-STAGE PROCESS

Expert system development is normally described as being evolutionary, incremental or iterative. The emphasis is on developing a rapid prototype of a system which undergoes a number of improving versions.

In abstract terms, the method has been described as a five-stage process (Hayes-Roth *et al.*, 1983):

1. Identification. During identification the knowledge engineer and expert work

44

together to identify the problem area, define its scope and identify the resources needed for the project.
2. Conceptualization. During conceptualization, the expert and knowledge engineer explicate the key concepts and relationships needed to describe the 'expertise' in a given domain.
3. Formalization. This involves mapping the concepts and relationships into a formal representation suggested by some expert system building tool or language.
4. Implementation. During implementation the knowledge engineer combines and reorganizes the formal knowledge in order to define a prototype system capable of being executed and tested.
5. Testing. This involves evaluating the performance of the prototype in terms of a set of standards usually defined by the domain expert.

Let us consider the important parts of each of these five stages in more detail.

5.2.1 Identification

Before developing an expert system, it is important to describe with as much precision as possible the problem the system is intended to solve. This is the first stage of knowledge elicitation or acquisition. Identification involves eliciting the generalities of the knowledge domain.

The knowledge engineer is usually unlikely to be familiar with the area under study. His first task is therefore to gain some familiarity with the domain. This normally involves such background research as consulting a range of knowledge sources – manuals, training guides, etc.

The primary knowledge elicitation technique is, however, the face-to-face interview usually organized around a discussion of problem-solving activity. In such an interview, which is usually recorded, the domain expert is often requested to outline several typical problem situations or cases. The results of the interview are then transcribed. The knowledge engineer analyses this interview material, attempting to extract some fundamental concepts in order to develop a general notion of the overall purpose of the expert system.

The knowledge engineer documents this general conception as an initial specification of the problem. Typically, this first attempt is inadequate in the sense that it does not entirely represent the generalities of the problem. The domain expert hopefully suggests changes to the specification and provides the knowledge engineer with additional case material to further refine the problem description.

Having used this material to revise the specification document, the knowledge engineer presents it to the domain expert for further suggestions. This process is repeated until the domain expert is happy that the specification document adequately describes, at least at a high level, the problem the expert system is designed to solve.

This iterative, incremental or evolutionary process is characteristic, first, of each of the stages of expert system development, and second, of the relationship between the various stages of the development process.

5.2.2 Conceptualization

In the identification stage, the knowledge engineer makes sure he understands the generalities of the problem. In the conceptualization stage, he turns his attention to the specifics of the problem. This normally means that interviews become more focused and the analysis of the interview material becomes more detailed. The knowledge engineer now attempts to split up the problem into manageable parts. He attempts to identify the structure of the knowledge domain in terms of concepts and the relationships between concepts.

5.2.3 Formalization

In the identification and conceptualization stages the idea is simply to understand the problem. During the formalization stage the problem is connected to its proposed solution by mapping the key concepts and relationships into more formal representations based upon the various knowledge-engineering tools and frameworks.

During this stage it is therefore important that the knowledge engineer be familiar with the various techniques of knowledge representation and inference used in the field. Likewise, it is important that he knows something of the available tools, languages and environments. Finally, it is useful to know of any other expert systems that solve similar problems and that hence may be adapted to the problem at hand.

5.2.4 Implementation

Implementation involves mapping the knowledge of the formalization stage into the representational framework associated with the tool chosen for the problem-solution. The overall idea is to construct an initial prototype of the expert system.

Once such a prototype is built, the next step is to evaluate its performance in order to determine whether the techniques chosen were the right ones for the job. If they are found to be incorrect or unmanageable then the prototype will be revised or even redone.

5.2.5 Testing

The chances of a validated prototype executing flawlessly first time are very slim. The testing stage is therefore designed to identify the key weaknesses in the construction of the expert system prior to making appropriate amendments. Testing usually begins by running a number of straightforward test-cases on the system. Once the knowledge engineer is satisfied that these execute correctly, more complex test-material which requires more human expertise is run on the system. This incremental testing continues until the results offered by the expert system sufficiently match with those proposed by the domain expert.

5.3 KNOWLEDGE ENGINEERING AND SOFTWARE ENGINEERING

Those readers with some background in conventional information systems work should see some obvious similarities between the methodology described for building expert systems and that process normally described in software engineering as the systems development life-cycle.

Identification and conceptualization are two high-level activities undertaken by every system analyst. Formalization is really systems design under another guise. Implementation and testing are processes common to both knowledge engineering and software engineering.

The relationship between traditional software development and expert systems development is characterized by two opposing positions. On the one hand we have the negative viewpoint expressed in such terms as:

> There really isn't much to say about this new profession of knowledge engineering. It appears to be another case of glamorising the familiar with pretentious new terminology. (Martins, 1984)

On the other hand we have the positive viewpoint:

> Can Artificial Intelligence technology be applied to software engineering, and in particular to the systems analysis stage of software development? I shall argue . . . that it can, and that in some cases Artificial Intelligence can render systems analysis efficient enough to remove the need for separate specifications and programs. (Kowalski, 1984)

5.3.1 Knowledge engineering: the negative viewpoint

The negative viewpoint usually runs as follows:

1. Expert systems development costs are high, development times are long, and the resulting systems consume large amounts of computing resources.
2. This tends to lead one to think that knowledge engineering methodologies are effective only for small and relatively simple applications. For applications of any real complexity, expert systems software is generally hard to understand, debug and maintain.
3. In more general terms, knowledge engineering has been described as a scientific cul-de-sac which diverts attention from the more important and deeper questions of AI (White, 1987).

In short, expert systems are at best either a re-invention of the wheel obscured by a new and fashionable jargon, or at worst a dead end which is diverting scarce resources from more important issues.

5.3.2 Knowledge engineering: the positive viewpoint

In contrast, the positive viewpoint runs something like:

1. Knowledge engineering in the large is frequently seen as being uneconomic only because it is still in its infancy. With the development of new machines and software not tied to the traditional Von-Neumann architecture, knowledge engineering will become a much more feasible and prevalent occupation.
2. The new software technologies not only allow the development of new applications in areas like expert systems but also facilitate the building of traditional software

applications. For instance, Kowalski (1984) has argued that logic-based applications can be thought of as executable analyses or specifications, thus removing the commonplace distinction between specification and program. As an extension to this argument it has been suggested that an expert systems methodology based around the notions of evolutionary development and rapid prototyping is a more effective development model than the traditional waterfall methodology of software engineering.

3. In general terms, the implementation of knowledge base systems is a more encompassing and promising solution to the software development bottleneck than that proposed under the aegis of software engineering.

At this extreme therefore we may sum up this position as suggesting that knowledge engineering offers much future promise for producing better computer systems.

5.3.3 Knowledge engineering: the middle viewpoint

The truth, as usual, probably lies somewhere in between these two extreme positions. Undoubtedly, the claims made for knowledge engineering, much like the early claims made for AI (see Chapter 12), have been over-inflated. Nevertheless, the innovatory nature of expert systems work in particular and AI work in general are having, and must eventually have, a profound impact on the traditional software development process.

A middle viewpoint might therefore be summarized as follows. There are clear connections between expert systems work and traditional systems development. This is particularly true if we examine the notion of building expert systems as being a process of iterative or evolutionary development centred around the production of prototypes. The rationale behind prototyping holds both for software engineering and knowledge engineering, namely that many users/domain experts simply do not know what to expect from a computer system. It is only by producing something for them to work with that they become able to express their true requirements or expertise.

Knowledge engineering, by its very nature, is frequently an experimental exercise. Many experts have never really been called upon to think upon or explicate what goes into making them expert. Encouraging such persons to engage in this kind of thinking and explication is extremely difficult without a point of focus. Such a focus is provided by a series of developed prototypes.

Considering users rather than domain experts does not, however, substantially change the picture. Most software development has at least a little of the original and experimental incorporated within it. The only major difference lies in the fact that most current software development works within a constrained arena of well-defined, well-studied and well-structured categories. Stock control, order-processing and sales ledger applications, to name but a few, have been well studied since the early years of commercial computing. Software engineers know how to build such systems in the sense that connections have been made between suitable methods and given problems.

In contrast, knowledge engineering is still an immature discipline in the sense that as yet it has not built up a corpus of methodological expertise. The discipline has not as yet had sufficient time to demonstrate appropriate amounts of method–problem connections. Although the summary description of the much-quoted methodology of Hayes-Roth *et al.* given earlier is a useful first step, there is still much detail to be filled in. The existing knowledge engineering literature still has much to say, for instance, about appropriate ways of documenting knowledge.

5.4 RAPID PROTOTYPING

As we indicated in Section 5.2, knowledge base system development is normally described as being evolutionary, incremental or iterative. The emphasis is on developing a rapid prototype which undergoes a number of improving versions.

Rapid prototyping has been a much-used technique over the last few years in traditional software development (Hayes-Roth *et al.*, 1983). This section examines some of the lessons learned in this endeavour as a basis for making a case for a clearer application of a structured approach to the development of expert systems.

5.4.1 What is prototyping?

Prototyping is essentially the process of building a system in an iterative way. Normally using an expert system shell, the knowledge engineer constructs a working model which he demonstrates to the domain expert. He and the expert then discuss the prototype, agreeing on enhancement and amendments. The ease of use of most shells means that the knowledge engineer can quickly make the suggested improvements in the working model. This cycle of inspection–discussion–amendment is repeated several times until the expert is satisfied with the system.

5.4.2 Benefits of prototyping

Prototyping allows the expert to refine his ideas on what the system should look like. Prototyping allows experts to be wrong. The fact that experts can change their minds is a recognized and encouraged part of the process. As a result of this, the knowledge engineer gets a better understanding of what the expert wants, and the knowledge engineer gets a clearer idea of the knowledge in the domain. The primary objective of prototyping in knowledge engineering is to clarify expertise. Prototyping eliminates surprises at the end of the development cycle, as users and experts have seen and agreed what will be delivered.

5.4.3 Problems with prototyping

The major problem with prototyping lies in identifying precisely what it is. In knowledge engineering it is used as the basis for system production. In software engineering it is used mainly as a vehicle for system specification.

The latter view of prototyping is prevalent in many other professions, e.g. mechanical engineering. It is taken for granted in mechanical engineering that the prototype will eventually be thrown away. In software engineering, there is much discussion as to whether the prototype should itself become part of the final system.

If the implementation tool being used is sufficiently powerful and flexible to make lower-level coding unnecessary, there may be a strong case for effectively implementing a prototype. What often happens, however, is that prototyping initiates the 'prefab' problem; i.e. because the user wants the system quickly, the prototype is implemented on a temporary basis. Many important things are left undone, e.g. proper recovery and restart procedures, proper test planning, proper sizing, etc. As with post-war prefab housing, the intention is to replace the prototype with something more substantial quite soon. However, because of other issues, the implemented prototype, with all its pressing problems, remains in production.

The nature of prototyping, where documentation follows on from the model, rather than coming before it, means that there is also the risk of a prototype continuing into production undocumented. Associated with this is the problem that large-scale proto-types can become unmanageable through repeated iterations. The lack of documentation and repeated changes can so affect the system that the time taken to make further changes increases unacceptably.

Over a period of years, the cumulative effect of modifications to a traditional system can make the implementation of further changes harder and harder as the initial sound structure of the system becomes more and more compromised. A prototype taken through to implementation may show similar characteristics, as it has been subject to repeated change during development. The difference is that the system derived from a prototype is already several years 'old' when implemented.

Perhaps the greatest problem, however, is that, due to the open-ended nature of the exercise, there is great difficulty in providing accurate estimating and resource planning for prototyping. This is a serious problem given that most commercial software projects have to justify themselves financially.

5.4.4 Effective prototyping

The problems with prototyping have forced many persons to the conclusion that prototyping should never be used instead of good project management. Prototyping may well alter the project life-cycle, especially because it facilitates iterative improvement. What it does not do is replace the project life-cycle. There is still a need for strong project management and the application of a structured systems analysis and design methodology.

The Central Communications and Technological Agency (CCTA) of the British Civil Service made the following comment on this issue a number of years ago:

> Experiments with the (expert systems) technology should be directed towards . . . starting to formulate a methodology for developing, monitoring and controlling expert systems projects, and addressing how this would relate to existing approaches (such as PROMPT and SSADM) and the existing organizational structure for handling information technology projects. (CCTA, 1986)

This conclusion is particularly important for knowledge engineering because of the fact that traditional expert systems development costs are high, and development times are long. This has led many people to feel that knowledge engineering methodologies are effective only for small and relatively simple applications. For applications of any real complexity, expert systems software is generally felt to be hard to understand, debug and maintain (Martins, 1984; White, 1987).

5.5 KNOWLEDGE ENGINEERING AND STRUCTURED DEVELOPMENT

The case behind this chapter is founded on two major premises. The first premise is that knowledge base systems will never be commercially viable until we learn to develop them on time and within budget, just as we do with conventional systems (Bonnet, 1988). Structured systems development methods are the key to doing this, just as they are in more traditional systems implementation.

Structured systems analysis and design are built up of a series of well-defined stages in the project life cycle: selection, feasibility, analysis, design, implementation, evaluation, and maintenance. Each of these stages is subject to a high degree of internal validation in terms of products and procedures. The relationships between stages are also subject to a great deal of external validation, in the sense that the inputs and outputs from each stage are well defined and hence amenable to rigorous checking.

Rapid prototyping is a structured technique in the sense that first, there are definable, repeatable steps in the process and, second, a higher-level design such as the user interface drives the lower-level programming process such as file or knowledge base manipulation. Rapid prototyping, however, has often been the only system development technique used to build expert systems. Little attempt has been made to introduce the extensive preliminary planning and design so familiar to traditional system developers. This is acceptable and even desirable in a laboratory environment founded on the principles of research and experimentation. It is unacceptable in the business world founded on the principles of development and cost.

It is suggested, then, that rigorous examples exist in conventional systems analysis and design, and that these proven approaches can be adapted to developing expert systems. This is particularly applicable in the area of documenting the initial functional requirements for an expert system. For example, data-flow diagrams, a traditional systems analysis tool, can be used to describe the flow of information in the problem domain. Also, a technique such as entity–relationship diagramming can be extended and used to document the concepts in a domain and the relationships between such concepts (see Chapter 9). However, not only the techniques but the whole framework of structured systems development can be adapted to knowledge engineering.

The major difference between this approach and that traditionally advocated for expert systems development is that it forces two important barriers between the analysis and design stages, and the design and implementation stages of the systems development cycle. The knowledge engineer still uses rapid prototyping as a means of eliciting the domain expertise, but this expertise is explicitly documented in a number of other ways than simply in the form of a rule base. The 'requirements document' is then used to explicitly design the finalized system. The design may actually be a simple re-jigging of the developed prototype. It may, however, often involve the complete re-design of the knowledge base in the light of the experience gained. This design document is then used to implement the finalized system (De-Salvo *et al.*, 1987).

The main advantage of constraining prototyping in this way is that it is a means of ensuring that the knowledge base is portable – i.e. machine- and tool-independent. It could be that the industrial user of the proposed expert system decides to use the knowledge base in a form other than that of an expert system. They may, for instance, decide to use it as an embedded piece of software in a traditional system (Maney and

Reid, 1986), or even as a set of manual procedures. A structured approach to analysis and design enables this by building up a conceptual or logical model of a system which may then be implemented in a number of different ways.

Another advantage is that methods that emulate those used in conventional information systems development stimulate connectivity between knowledge base systems and conventional information systems. Methods based on a structured approach are far easier to manage in terms of estimating the time and resources needed to be devoted to a project. It is also far easier to justify an expert system project in classic cost-benefit terms using a structured approach.

The second major premise of this chapter, then, is that structured analysis and design techniques can permit expert systems development to proceed with essentially the same regularity of effort and predictability that exemplify conventional systems development.

5.6 DEVELOPMENT METHODOLOGIES FOR EXPERT SYSTEMS

Some work has already taken place in proposing structured methodologies for knowledge base system development. This area has expanded over the last few years (Hilal and Soltan, 1991). A number of approaches have been suggested by organizations funded by the European research initiative ESPRIT and the British research initiative Alvey:

- KADS (Knowledge Acquisition and Documentation Structuring)
- KEMRAS (Knowledge Elicitation Methodology for Research Associations)
- POMESS (A People Oriented Methodology for Expert Systems)
- SOCRATES (An Automated Logical Methodology)

The USA has also been actively involved in methodology development. NASA, for instance, has been an active participant in the field through the Hubble Space Telescope Design/Engineering Knowledge Base Projects (HSTDEK). Also, various commercial institutions have suggested their own methods.

Such methodologies vary enormously in their level of detail and orientation. Some methods, such as HSTDEK, are designed for large projects. Others, such as POMESS, are oriented primarily to the user. Methodologies like KEMRAS are concerned mainly with the problems of knowledge elicitation. Others such as KADS impose an entire life-cycle on the development process.

5.6.1 KADS

Probably the foremost of these efforts is a methodology known usually by the acronym KADS. KADS originally stood for Knowledge Acquisition and Documentation Structuring. It is now also referred to as Knowledge Analysis and Design System. KADS is the result of a six-year ESPRIT-sponsored collaborative research and development effort between four European countries. Hickman (1989) estimates that over 70 man-years of effort have been invested in the project. He also makes the claim that, 'the KADS methodology is set to become the de-facto standard for KBS development in the UK and within Europe'.

KADS uses a development life-cycle very similar to the conventional software development life-cycle. The KADS life-cycle consists of the following stages:

1. Analysis
2. Design
3. Implementation
4. Installation
5. Use
6. Maintenance
7. Knowledge refinement

Each phase is defined in terms of the activities which occur in the phase and the outputs produced. Fig. 5.1 provides an overview of the KADS life-cycle.

The most significant differences between KADS and conventional software development occur at the analysis stage. It is not surprising, therefore, that the analysis phase has received the most attention in the literature.

KADS takes an explicit modelling approach to expert system development. An expert system in KADS is a model of some problem-solving expertise. The cornerstone of KADS analysis is a generic model of such expertise which is used to drive the knowledge elicitation process. KADS provides a library of generic models that describe the ideal–typical characteristics of various distinct types of problem-solving activity (Hayball and Barlow, 1990). We defer discussion of this process until Chapter 8.

In this work we shall use a framework for the expert system development life-cycle which is very similar to that proposed by KADS. There are, however, some points of difference:

1. We include in the next chapter some explicit discussion of selecting expert system projects and assessing their feasibility.

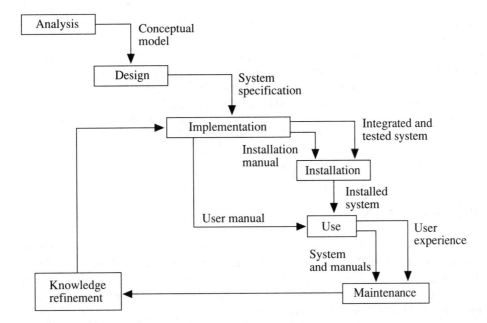

Figure 5.1 Overview of the KADS life-cycle.

2. KADS takes a specific approach to building expert systems based upon the use of generic models of problem-solving. Although this is useful in driving the process of knowledge capture, it does not give us any clear idea of how expert system technology can merge with conventional software.
3. We have therefore chosen to directly adapt some of the techniques from conventional systems development to the needs of knowledge engineering.

5.7 CONCLUSION

Faden has cast the expert systems methodology debate into an antagonism between those from traditional software development backgrounds, and those brought up solely in the environment of the new technology (Faden, 1986). There is undoubtedly a lot of truth in this analysis at the personal level. At the level of the discipline as a whole, however, it does not remove the fact that since expert systems are becoming a commercial proposition, they are going to meet with the same exigencies as those imposed upon conventional software.

In fact, it is the author's belief that what we are probably seeing here is the gradual movement of the term 'conventional software' to encompass the whole area of knowledge base systems (Beynon-Davies, 1987, 1991). As such, debates about the relevance of traditional methods to knowledge engineering and indeed the application of knowledge engineering to software engineering are an important part of the encompassing process.

5.8 RECALL EXERCISES

1. What is meant by conceptualization in the context of the methodology proposed by Hayes-Roth *et al.*?
2. Describe the rapid prototyping approach to knowledge base system development.
3. What are the advantages and disadvantages of the prototyping approach?
4. Describe the negative viewpoint on knowledge engineering.
5. Describe the positive viewpoint on knowledge engineering.
6. Why has structured development been seen as beneficial to commercial KBS development?
7. What is KADS?
8. Describe the life-cycle proposed by KADS.

5.9 OPEN-ENDED EXERCISES

1. Benyon and Skidmore (1987) have criticized the trend towards developing competing methodologies in conventional systems work. They consider it unlikely that any single methodology will be able to prescribe how to tackle the great variety of tasks and situations experienced by the conventional systems developer. Discuss this viewpoint in the context of knowledge base systems work.
2. In this chapter we have mainly discussed the links between software engineering and

knowledge engineering. In recent times, a new branch of business computing – information engineering – has arisen. Martin (1984) defines information engineering as 'the set of interrelated disciplines which are needed to build a computerized enterprise based on data systems. The primary focus of information engineering is on the data that are stored and maintained by computers and the information that is distilled from these data'. Discuss information engineering in the context of knowledge engineering.

3. The idea of evolutionary development has become influential in some quarters of information systems work. Evolutionary development embodies the idea of building a system by small, incremental steps, each of which forms a working system. Discuss whether evolutionary development might be an appropriate approach for knowledge engineering.

REFERENCES

Benyon D. and Skidmore S. (1987). Towards a toolkit for the systems analyst. *Computer Journal*, **30**(11), 57–73.

Beynon-Davies P. (1987). Software engineering and knowledge engineering: unhappy bedfellows? *Computer Bulletin*, December.

Beynon-Davies P. (1991). *Expert Database Systems: A Gentle Introduction*. McGraw-Hill, London.

C.C.T.A. (1986). *Expert Systems: Some Guidelines*. London.

De Salvo D.A., Glamm A.E. and Liebowitz J. (1987). Structured design of an expert system prototype at the National Archives. In Barry G. Silverman (Ed.) *Expert Systems for Business*. Addison-Wesley, Reading, MA.

Faden M. (1986). What do you want in a knowledge engineer? *Expert Systems User*, September.

Hayball C. and Barlow D. (1990). Skills support in the ICL (Kidsgrove) Bonding Shop – a case study in the application of the KADS methodology. In Berry D. and Hart A. (Eds) *Expert Systems: Human Aspects*. Chapman and Hall, London.

Hayes-Roth F., Waterman D. and Lenat D.B. (Eds.) (1983). *Building Expert Systems*. Addison-Wesley, Reading, MA.

Hickman F. (Ed.) (1989). *Knowledge Based Systems Analysis: A Pragmatic Introduction to the KADS Methodology*. Ellis Horwood, Cambridge.

Hilal D.K. and Soltan H. (1991). A suggested descriptive framework for the comparison of knowledge-based systems methodologies. *Expert Systems* **8**(2), 107–114.

Kowalski R. (1984). AI and software engineering. *Datamation* **30**(18), 21–28.

Maney T. and Reid I. (1986). *A Management Guide to Artificial Intelligence*. Paradigm, London.

Martin J. (1984). *An Information Systems Manifesto*. Prentice-Hall, Englewood-Cliffs, NJ.

Martins G.R. (1984). The overselling of expert systems. *Datamation* **30**(18), 30–32.

White I. (1987). W(h)ither expert systems. *BCS Specialist Group on Expert Systems Newsletter* 17.

PROJECT SELECTION

6.1 INTRODUCTION

The first two stages in a scheme for the structured development of knowledge base systems we shall call the *project selection* stage and the *feasibility study*.

These stages are two 'filters' at the front of the project life-cycle, designed to weed out those applications unsuitable for knowledge base development (Fig. 6.1). The project selection process is a coarse-grained filter. It is designed to answer the general question, when is a particular application suitable for the knowledge base approach? In contrast, the feasibility study is a fine-grained filter. It is designed to answer more detailed questions such as which particular expert system projects should be undertaken by a particular enterprise.

This chapter primarily deals with the more general questions of project selection. Because of the dependence of the feasibility study on the project selection process, however, a certain amount of the material discussed here is of equal relevance to this fine-grained filter.

It is possible to distinguish between at least two methods for selecting expert system projects. The first approach is based on a series of properties which the stereotypical, successful expert system project possesses—this we shall call the checklist approach. The second, which we shall call the business analysis approach, is directed towards identifying suitable business areas for expert systems work.

6.2 THE CHECKLIST APPROACH

It is possible to assess the appropriateness of an application for knowledge base

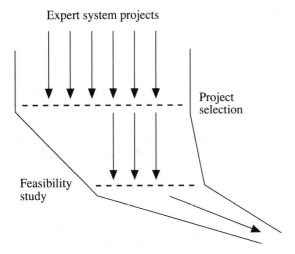

Expert system projects

Project selection

Feasibility study

Figure 6.1   The first two stages of knowledge base system development.

development by inferencing on the following knowledge base in a backward-chaining manner (Silverman, 1987).

GOAL knowledge base_approach

IF project_relevance is likely
AND project_feasibility is likely
AND project_desirability is likely
AND project_success is likely
THEN knowledge base_approach is appropriate

IF skilled_employees are rare
OR knowledge is distributed
OR complex_problems are common
OR high_training_levels are normal
AND problem_occurrence is regular
AND problem_solution is reasonably_quick
THEN project_relevance is likely

IF domain_experts are available
AND regular_consultation is feasible
AND domain_knowledge is uncontroversial
AND knowledge_representation is feasible
THEN project_feasibility is likely

IF heuristics are applicable
AND uncertainty is applicable
AND explanation is important
THEN project_desirability is likely

```
IF problem__solutions are high__value
AND management__support is likely
AND test__data is plentiful
AND iterative__development is feasible
AND development__team is competent
AND structured__development is used
THEN project__success is likely
```

The top-level rule identifies four important factors: relevance, feasibility, desirability and success. Each of the lower-level rules provide more detail on each of these factors. We examine each factor in turn.

6.2.1 Relevance

The relevance rule states first, that the problem under consideration for development should be a routine one which is genuinely useful to the organization. A useful problem is, for instance, one which involves the codification and dissemination of some enterprise knowledge which is normally the prerogative of a small, overworked group of company employees. In this scenario, a knowledge base system can usefully act as 'insurance' against the loss of vital personnel.

Other yardsticks of usefulness are more temporal in nature. For instance, a system that is wheeled into action every few weeks to tackle a small subset of a complex problem is often not acceptable. This usually means that problems which take less than a few minutes of an expert's time to solve are probably not worth addressing, neither are problems which take days of concentrated effort. The former is probably too trivial a problem for an expert system application: the latter is probably too complex for the present generation of software. This means that the ideal problem normally takes from an hour to a few hours to solve by a domain expert.

6.2.2 Feasibility

The question of feasibility at the project selection stage is largely a question of general company resources. We have to be certain, for instance, that the domain knowledge for the application is readily accessible in terms of our ability to interview domain experts. Such knowledge must also, however, be relatively well defined. There must be some form of agreement among the domain experts as to the corpus of the knowledge in the domain. If there is, for instance, wide disagreement about the components of a particular domain, then we are unlikely to be able to build a satisfactory system to represent that domain. Finally, we have to be fairly sure that the knowledge can be represented within the constraints of some existing development tool.

6.2.3 Desirability

Expert systems are often contrasted with more conventional software in their ability to operate in a heuristic rather than an algorithmic manner. A heuristic is a rule of thumb or an instance of 'good practice' in some domain. Unlike an algorithm, which is a step-by-step procedure for solving a particular problem, a heuristic does not guarantee a solution.

Expert systems are also characterized by two other exceptional characteristics: first, their ability to handle uncertain, erroneous and fuzzy data; and second, their ability to explain their reasoning.

The present generation of expert systems are primarily interactive tools. They most neatly fit under the conventional category of management information systems. In such systems, the ability to question the reasoning of the system is of primary importance. The user must be able to request explanations of the system in terms of how it arrived at a particular conclusion.

These characteristics tend to define expert systems as mechanisms for mopping up the exceptions that conventional systems cannot handle.

6.2.4 Success

The task the system is designed to solve must have a relatively high payoff for the organization. Since the effort needed to develop a useful knowledge base system is likely to be substantial, one must be sure that the benefits from the system are equally substantial.

We discussed in Chapter 5 how the development of an expert system is really nothing more than another software development effort. As such, it is subject to the same critical success factors as more conventional software. First and foremost, top management involvement is essential to ensure success. Management must be involved in the approval, direction and evaluation of any corporate knowledge engineering exercise. Second, it is essential that an experienced and highly motivated team is available for the development of the application. It has also been stressed that numerous advantages arise from the use of a structured methodology for systems development.

6.3 THE BUSINESS ANALYSIS APPROACH

The checklist approach can be used as a systematic method for expert systems project selection. For the method to work, however, there must already be an established set of projects to assess. The advantage of the business analysis approach is that it provides guidelines for pinpointing areas within a business which may have the potential for expert systems development.

This approach focuses on the decision-making processes within organizations. It exploits a distinction originally made by H.A. Simon between structured and unstructured decisions (Simon, 1977). A decision is structured if the decision-making process can be described in detail before the decision is made. Examples of structured decisions are *calculating an employees' tax contribution, pricing normal orders*, etc. A decision is unstructured if the decision-making process cannot be described in detail. This may be because the problem has not arisen before, is characterized by incomplete or uncertain knowledge, or uses non-quantifiable data, etc. Examples of unstructured decisions are *selecting personnel, estimating bespoke projects, or planning a production schedule* (Stow *et al.*, 1988).

The structured/unstructured distinction is not a hard and fast one. It is better seen as a continuum from the definitely structured (algorithmic) to the definitely unstructured (heuristic). In general, however, one can say that the decisions of greatest import to

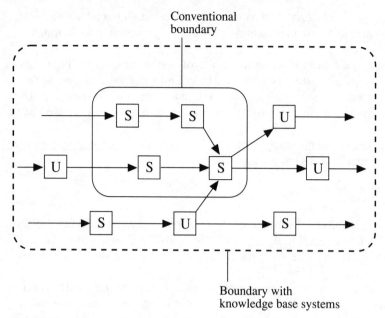

Figure 6.2 Structured and unstructured decision-making areas.

business organizations are unstructured. This is because the higher up the organization hierarchy one looks, the more likely are decisions to be unstructured (Sviokla, 1986).

At present, computers are largely used by businesses to support relatively structured decision-making areas such as payroll, accounts, order-processing and stock control. With the advent of expert systems, computer technology can now be applied to unstructured decision-making areas at the vertical and horizontal margins of information systems.

Figure 6.2 shows a diagram of part of the activities of an organization. This diagram is a data-flow diagram – a technique we shall discuss in some detail in Chapter 9. The boxes on the diagram represent processes. The arrows represent data flowing between processes. Any decisions which take place in the organization take place within processes. This means that we can roughly categorize processes as being structured (S) or unstructured (U). The layout of processes means that the present boundary of computerization is indicated by the bold line. If expert systems technology is available, then the boundary of computerization can be extended outwards to include newer, unstructured decision-making. As a consequence, further structured processes are now also brought into play. This is indicated by the dotted line.

The business analysis approach is similar to the framework proposed by Liebenau and Backhouse for information systems which we discussed in Chapter 2 (Liebenau and Backhouse, 1990). They portray organizations as having three major information dimensions: a technical dimension, a formal dimension and an informal dimension. Figure 6.3 illustrates these dimensions in terms of nested boxes. Technical information systems, of which computerized information systems are a part, are normally built within

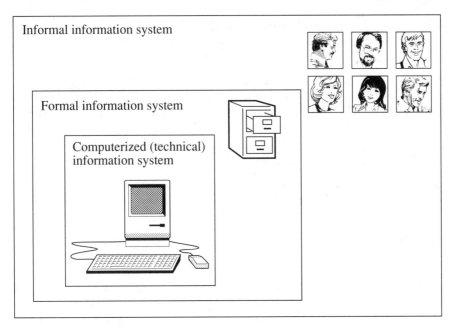

Figure 6.3 Informal, formal and technical information systems.

relatively well-defined boundaries of the formal information systems of organizations. Formal information systems are systems of defined rules, regulations and procedures. Informal information systems, in contrast, are characterized by less well-defined entities: norms, values and beliefs. Informal information systems, however, provide the context for formal systems; they define their scope and use.

Expert systems work is characterized by an attempt to increase the area of computing relevance from the purely formal domain into the realms of the informal. Expert systems are best seen as semi-formal information systems.

The computerization of the semi-formal may offer numerous opportunities for business organizations to improve their market share. Over the last decade, for example, the idea of using database systems for competitive advantage has proven successful (Beynon-Davies, 1991). Recently, companies have started to consider how the more encompassing concept of a knowledge base system can be used to direct the strategic and tactical decision-making of a company.

Newquist (1990) gives a number of examples of how the US retail sector is successfully applying expert systems technology. A purveyor of choice cookies, for instance, has developed a host of integrated expert system modules which provide its store managers with accurate analyses of business conditions, projections as to the amount of cookies to be produced each day, and suggestions as to marketing strategies.

6.4 AN EXAMPLE OF PROJECT SELECTION

In this section we shall start considering one relatively simple expert systems project.

Personal Pensions Background

July 1988 saw British banks, building societies and unit trust groups being given the right to join insurance companies in providing pensions.

There are a number of categories of pension scheme available in Britain. Every person who worked in the UK used to pay a contribution to the state earnings related pension scheme (SERPS). As from July 1988, however, people were given the right to opt out from this scheme and pay their contribution into a scheme specific to some company (company pension scheme) or a scheme specifically designed for the individual (personal pension).

The CYMRO building society were one of a number of financial institutions who set up a personal pension facility in response to this legislation.

Figure 6.4   Background to personal pension system project.

This case study will be used to illustrate some of the issues, methods and techniques discussed in the main body of text. It is meant to portray the life-cycle of a typical commercial expert systems project. The application is from the financial services sector: a personal pension quotation system. Fig. 6.4 documents the background to the personal pension system project.

The Cymro building society is one of a number of financial institutions that set up a personal pension facility in response to the legislation discussed in Fig. 6.4. The system at Cymro, however, is primarily a manual system fed initially by one of two forms:

1. Customer information form. This is filled in by a member of staff at one of Cymro's numerous branches as a result of an interview with the customer. It is then posted to head office.
2. Pension enquiry form. This is filled in by the customer himself and then posted either to the customer's local branch or to head office. If the customer sends the form to the local branch, this is re-routed to head office.

The customer information and pension enquiry forms are illustrated in Fig. 6.5.

Once a form is received at head office by a small team of one personal pension expert and two clerical staff, the following steps take place:

1. The branch to be responsible for the customer is determined, usually from the customer's postcode.
2. Using the customer information supplied, the appropriate pension plan is determined.
3. A detailed quotation is produced for the customer using a piece of application software previously written for Cymro.
4. A covering letter is produced. If the quotation is a standard case this letter is chosen from a number of standard letters stored on a word-processor. A non-standard case, however, requires staff to write a personal letter or to give advice to the local branch manager who responds to the customer.

```
                Personal Pensions
              Customer Information Form

  ┌──────────────┬─────────────────────────┐
  │ Branch       │ Date of Interview       │
  ├──────────────┼─────────────────────────┤
  │ Signed       │ Time of Interview       │
  └──────────────┴─────────────────────────┘

  ┌──────────┬─────────────┬────────────────┐
  │ Title    │ Date of birth│ Occupation    │
  ├──────────┴─────────────┼────────────────┤
  │ Surname               │ Sex            │
  ├────────────────────────┼────────────────┤
  │ Forenames             │ Marital Status │
  └────────────────────────┴────────────────┘

  ┌─────────────────────────────────────────┐
  │ Present Address                         │
  │                                         │
  ├──────────────┬──────────────────────────┤
  │ Postcode     │ Home Phone No            │
  │              ├──────────────────────────┤
  │              │ Business Phone No        │
  └──────────────┴──────────────────────────┘

  ┌──────────────────┬──────────────┬────────┐
  │ Non-pensionable  │ Highest Tax  │        │
  │ Income           │ Rate         │        │
  ├──────────────────┼──────────────┼────────┤
  │ Smoker           │ Existing Pension│Details│
  ├──────────────────┤ Arrangements │        │
  │ Good Health      │              │        │
  ├──────────────────┴──────────────┴────────┤
  │ Occupational Scheme Member               │
  ├──────────────────────────────────────────┤
  │ Contracted Out                           │
  ├──────────────────────────────────────────┤
  │ Preferred Retirement Age                 │
  ├──────────────────────────────────────────┤
  │ Need High Security                       │
  └──────────────────────────────────────────┘
```

```
                Personal Pensions
                  Enquiry Form
  Take this form into your local branch or post it today to:-
      The Cymro Pensions Service, Cymro Building Society, Cymro
      Tower, Fisherman's Wharf, Cardiff, CF41 8PU

  Please send me free details on a personal pension to suit me.

  BLOCK CAPITALS PLEASE

  ┌──────────────┬───────────────────────────┐
  │ Title        │ Name                      │
  └──────────────┴───────────────────────────┘

  ┌──────────────────────────────────────────┐
  │ Address                                  │
  │                                          │
  ├──────────────┬───────────────────────────┤
  │ Postcode     │ Daytime Phone No          │
  └──────────────┴───────────────────────────┘

  ┌──────────────────┬───────────────────────┐
  │ Date of birth    │ Sex                   │
  └──────────────────┴───────────────────────┘

  ┌──────────────────┬───────────────────────┐
  │ Salary           │ Age at which          │
  │                  │ I wish to retire      │
  └──────────────────┴───────────────────────┘

  So that we can select the pension plan most suited to your
  circumstances please tick the appropriate boxes below:

  Employed – not in a company scheme          ┌──────┐
  Employed – in a company scheme              └──────┘
  Are you currently in the State Earnings Related
  Pension Scheme (SERPS)?                   [yes] [no]
  Any known details of existing pension arrangements?

  Are you a Cymro account holder?           [yes] [no]

  Number of existing Cymro account
```

Figure 6.5 Customer information and pension enquiry forms.

Figure 6.6 documents the existing system as a data-flow diagram (a technique to be discussed in Chapter 9).

A number of problems exist in the current system:

1. Computer technology is used to automate a number of functions in the system. The software is disconnected, however; staff have to perform a number of separate steps using different application packages to produce a final response.
2. The expert devotes a great deal of time to determining the appropriate pension plans for customers. This leaves very little time for other important activities such as planning marketing strategy, etc.
3. When the expert is unavailable due to sickness or when he attends meetings, the processing of applications has to be temporarily suspended.

After a series of interviews with the expert it soon became apparent that something in the order of 70 per cent of enquiries fell into the category of standard cases. A standard case is one which the expert could detail with some certainty the appropriate outcome given the information provided by the customer. The aim of the proposed expert system is therefore to automate the handling of all the steps involved in producing standard quotations.

6.4.1 Selecting the project

Let us therefore place this proposed expert system in the context of the two frameworks we have described for selecting expert system projects: the checklist approach and the business analysis approach.

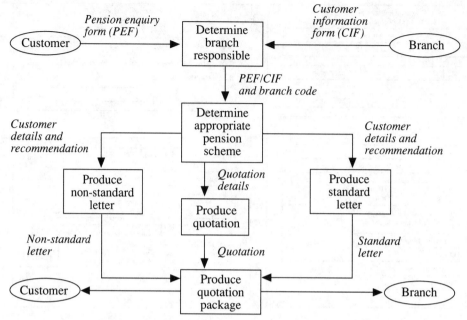

Figure 6.6   Data-flow diagram documenting Cymro's existing pension quotation system.

6.4.2 Checklist approach

The pension system is certainly relevant to the work of the Cymro building society. It involves disseminating the knowledge of an overworked pensions expert throughout Cymro. The problem of determining a pension is certainly a routine one, taking usually less than half an hour to solve.

The system is feasible. For standard cases the knowledge appears to be fairly well defined. The knowledge engineers have also been given access, albeit irregularly, to the appropriate domain expert.

The system is desirable. The application seems to demand the application of heuristics. Whether reasoning with uncertainty and explanation are required remains to be seen.

The system is likely to succeed. Freeing the pensions expert will be a cost saving. Disseminating the system to branches might improve the pensions business.

6.4.3 Business analysis

Each process box on the data-flow diagram in Fig. 6.6 can be labelled S for structured or U for unstructured. By doing this we can see that a number of relatively structured processes feed and are fed from one unstructured process (see Fig. 6.7). Automating this unstructured process is therefore clearly desirable if only on the grounds of integration.

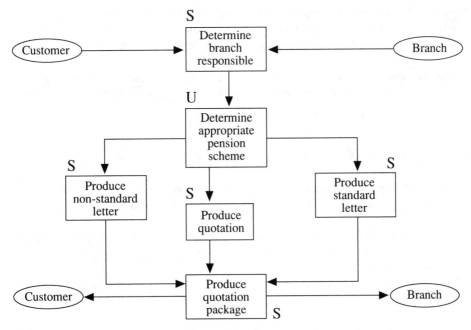

Figure 6.7 Structured and unstructured processes at Goronwy.

6.5 CONCLUSION

This chapter began by discussing the related nature of the selection of expert system projects and assessing the feasibility of such projects. Project selection is a coarse-grained filter, while the feasibility study is a fine-grained filter.

We then discussed two contrasting approaches to project selection: the checklist approach and the business analysis approach. The checklist approach is almost an expert system for selecting or appraising expert system proposals. The business analysis approach relies on the distinction between structured and unstructured decision-making.

These two approaches were applied to a simple case study. The general conclusion is that the personal pensions project looks eminently suitable for expert systems development.

The next two chapters are devoted to the process of acquiring, eliciting and documenting the knowledge relevant to a particular domain. We first consider the process of acquiring and eliciting knowledge. Then we consider the process of building a conceptual model of some domain. Both these processes are interdependent within the general context of knowledge analysis.

6.6 RECALL EXERCISES

1. Describe the difference between project selection and feasibility study.
2. Why is the checklist approach an expert system for project selection?

3. Describe the business analysis approach to selecting expert system projects.
4. What advantages arise from applying a business analysis approach?
5. Give three examples of structured and three examples of unstructured decision-making.
6. How might the checklist approach and the business analysis approach be combined?
7. In what way might we describe expert systems as being semi-formal information systems?

6.7 OPEN-ENDED EXERCISES

1. There is a tendency in organizations to attempt to transform as many unstructured decision-making areas as possible into structured decision-making areas. Discuss this tendency.
2. Many persons have discussed the crucial role of an 'expert systems champion' within organizations; that is, someone amenable to investigating and promulgating the use of expert systems. Discuss.
3. How important to the success of an expert systems project is a skilled team of knowledge engineers?

REFERENCES

Beynon-Davies P. (1991). *Relational Database Systems: A Pragmatic Approach*. Blackwell Scientific, Oxford.
Liebenau J. and Backhouse J. (1990). *Understanding Information: An Introduction*. Macmillan, London.
Newquist H.P. (1990). Experts at retail. *Datamation*, April, 53–56.
Silverman B.G. (Ed.) (1987). *Expert Systems for Business*. Addison-Wesley, Reading, MA.
Simon H.A. (1977). *The New Science of Management Decision*. Prentice-Hall, Englewood Cliffs, NJ.
Stow R., Lunn S. and Slatter P. (1988). How to identify business applications of expert systems. *2nd International Expert Systems Conference*, Brighton.
Sviokla J. (1986). Business implications of knowledge-based systems. *Database*, Summer and Fall.

7

KNOWLEDGE ANALYSIS I: KNOWLEDGE ACQUISITION AND ELICITATION

7.1 INTRODUCTION

Knowledge acquisition and elicitation is the process of locating, collecting and refining the knowledge relevant to a particular domain. This process is often referred to as the major bottleneck in the development of expert systems for a number of reasons:

1. It is extremely difficult.
2. It is time-consuming.
3. There are, as yet, no easy, effective and encompassing methods available for extracting the knowledge of a domain expert.

A figure of one rule per person-day debugged and installed in a knowledge base is usually held to be average progress in knowledge elicitation. This is particularly limiting for a class of software which is beginning to benefit the business world.

Why then, is it so difficult to extract knowledge from a domain expert? The answer probably lies in the fact that expertise is an ability which does not usually involve the capacity to explain reasoning. This is often referred to as the paradox of expertise. That is, the more competent people become in a particular knowledge domain, the less able they are to explain what goes into making them expert.

A number of researchers have begun, however, to exploit a facet of an expert's skill that they believe is more amenable to analysis. Namely, that although experts are often unable to explain their reasoning in detail, they are usually able to act as a fountainhead for a whole range of examples with which to train an apprentice. The apprentice in our terms is, of course, an item of software which takes these examples and induces a set of rules from them.

This chapter is therefore divided into two parts. In the first part we consider some of the issues surrounding the conventional, manual approach to knowledge acquisition and elicitation. In the second half, we discuss the idea of an automatic knowledge acquisition facility.

7.2 KNOWLEDGE ACQUISITION AND ELICITATION

The term *knowledge acquisition* is frequently used as a synonym for *knowledge elicitation*. However, some knowledge engineers prefer to distinguish between the two terms. Hickman (1989), for instance, prefers to reserve the term knowledge acquisition for all mechanisms used for gathering knowledge, whether it be from experts, users, books or manuals. In contrast, knowledge elicitation is specifically reserved for the gleaning of knowledge from domain experts. Because of the interdependence of these activities, we shall choose to use the terms knowledge acquisition and elicitation as relative synonyms.

The use of different knowledge sources is good practice in any knowledge analysis exercise. Frequently the results gained from one source will directly contradict the knowledge gleaned from other sources. A frequent occurrence is to find that 'textbook descriptions' of expertise in some area are either incomplete or erroneous. Collins (1990) cites an interesting case where the classic textbook on growing crystals in the laboratory lists methods which do not actually work in practice. Hence, although laboratory technicians told the knowledge engineer they were growing crystals in the prescribed manner, they were actually conducting the exercise by an entirely different procedure.

7.3 THE THREE STAGES OF KNOWLEDGE ELICITATION

Knowledge elicitation is often said to fall into at least three stages (Wellbank, 1983):

1. An initial structuring of the domain. This is a stage characterized by an initial analysis of the domain. The objective is to develop a preliminary sketch of the important concepts in the domain.
2. Producing a first working knowledge base. This stage involves taking the concepts and identifying relationships between the concepts.
3. Testing and debugging the knowledge base. This final stage involves correcting and possibly reorganizing the body of knowledge.

Knowledge elicitation is not therefore a discrete stage at the start of expert systems development. It is an exercise which continues throughout the development process, probably in an iterative manner characteristic of prototyping as discussed in Chapter 5. Indeed, the idea of knowledge elicitation is used to bundle together a whole range of issues that have been considered in conventional software development, at least for the purposes of explication, separately.

In this chapter we shall therefore concentrate on discussing the first two, 'traditional', stages of elicitation: the initial structuring of the domain, and the methods employed in extracting the knowledge relevant to some domain. In the next chapter we shall discuss a number of methods for documenting the results of elicitation as well as the KADS approach of model-driven elicitation. The question of testing, debugging and eventually maintaining a knowledge base system we shall discuss in Chapter 11.

7.4 STAGE ONE: GETTING THE BASIC STRUCTURE

This stage has been described as probably the most difficult aspect of the knowledge elicitation process. The classic method of knowledge elicitation is to locate a domain expert who excels in his field (a 'star' domain expert) and closet him in a room with a competent knowledge engineer for a substantial period of time. This method is not workable within the confines of the business world for a number of reasons:

1. 'Star' domain experts are usually overworked and consequently highly paid. They are therefore unlikely to be willing to devote large periods of time to the development of an expert system.
2. Domain knowledge is likely to be distributed rather than centralized. In other words, the knowledge may not be in the head of any one person. It may be dispersed among a large number of less-skilled experts.
3. The demands of rapid development within a business environment may mean that a team of knowledge engineers, rather than a single knowledge engineer, will need to be given responsibility for the project.

New methods need to be developed to cope with the exigencies of the business world. Grover (1986), for instance, has suggested that a series of documents should be produced to accompany knowledge acquisition. At the domain definition stage, the knowledge engineer is encouraged to produce a handbook containing at least:

1. A general problem description.
2. A bibliography of reference documents.
3. A glossary of terms.
4. A list of experts in the field.
5. Some reasonable performance metrics.
6. Descriptions of typical scenarios of reasoning.

What we are discussing here is largely a consequence of the movement of knowledge engineering from the academic into the business arena. In undertaking this move, knowledge engineering must demonstrate that it has changed from primarily a hand-craft into something which clearly deserves the term *engineering* in its title. Commercial software development in the guise of software and information engineering has been considering such issues for a number of years. Software engineering, for instance, has had to demonstrate appropriate ways of documenting systems and managing the project life-cycle. Knowledge engineering has some way to go in demonstrating such methods. The author will make suggestions around these concerns throughout the text. It should be borne in mind, however, that no clear conclusions have yet been reached on the subject.

7.5 STAGE TWO: GETTING AT THE KNOWLEDGE

This is the phase of knowledge elicitation in which detailed collection of knowledge takes place. The various methods discussed in the literature can be categorized under two major headings: the direct and the indirect approach. Direct methods expect the expert to be able to articulate or demonstrate the knowledge relevant to a particular domain. This set of methods includes interviews, questionnaires, simple observation and protocol analysis (Olson and Reuter, 1987). In contrast, indirect methods do not rely on an expert's ability to articulate about knowledge. Indirect methods collect other behaviours such as scaling responses. From this information the knowledge engineer can make inferences about what the expert must have known to respond in the way that he did. Indirect methods include such techniques as multi-dimensional scaling and repertory grid analysis.

7.5.1 Direct methods

Interviews Interviews are probably the most commonly used knowledge elicitation technique. In conversation, the expert is encouraged to reveal the objects he thinks are important, how they are related or organized, and some of the activities he undertakes in solving problems.

Questionnaires Interviews have the distinct advantage of being capable of extracting deep information about a particular knowledge domain. To do this, however, the technique is by its very nature time-consuming. Questionnaires, in contrast, are an extremely effective method of obtaining blanket, shallow coverage of some knowledge domain.

Simple observation Often the best way to discover how an expert solves a problem is to observe an expert in the process of undertaking a solution. Observation usually implies direct viewing of behaviour and taking notes on the spot. Many knowledge engineers have also videotaped activities in order to be able to perform more detailed analyses later.

Protocol analysis A close cousin to simple observation is protocol analysis. As with observation, the expert engages in performing a typical task. In addition, however, the expert is now expected to think out loud. In other words he is asked to describe what he is doing and why he is doing it.

   Direct techniques are characterized by a free and open format which enables the knowledge engineer to elicit many kinds of information – objects, relations, inference, rules, etc. All such direct techniques suffer, however, from the fact that experts cannot always express what they know or discuss how they solve a particular problem. Much of what constitutes a domain expert's knowledge may therefore be implicit.

7.5.2 Indirect methods

Indirect techniques are more limited in what they reveal, but may be more effective at eliciting implicit relationships between objects in some domain. Having said this, all such direct techniques make assumptions about the underlying representation of objects and relationships.

Multi-dimensional scaling In this method the expert is asked to make a series of similarity judgements on all pairs of objects or concepts in the domain of enquiry. For instance, how similar is a prudent pension to an equitable pension? The technique therefore assumes that such objects have been identified perhaps through a direct technique such as interviewing. These judgements are then laid out in a similarity matrix. The matrix is used as input to a program which lays out the items in a two-dimensional graphic representation of the distances between objects.

Repertory grid analysis This technique is comprehensive in that it includes an initial dialogue with the expert, a rating session, and an analysis which clusters objects along dimensions. The initial session begins with an open interview with the expert. The objective of this session is to get him or her to name some of the objects in the domain. Once a small set of objects is generated, the knowledge engineer picks three such objects and asks, 'what trait can be used to distinguish any two of these objects from the third?' The expert names some dimension, and then indicates which objects are 'high' and 'low' on this dimension. The knowledge engineer then assigns a scale-value (e.g. 1–3) to the three objects. This process of discriminating between triples continues until the analyst is satisfied that he has uncovered all the major dimensions of similarity/dissimilarity in the domain.

The knowledge engineer then constructs a grid. Objects are listed across the top, and dimensions are listed down the side. The expert is asked to rate all the objects on all the dimensions using some appropriate scale. This grid is then fed into two further analyses: one clusters the objects in terms of 'distances', the other clusters dimensions in the domain (Olson and Reuter, 1987).

7.6 AUTOMATIC KNOWLEDGE ACQUISITION

The idea of programming a computer to learn effective behaviour is at least as old as AI itself. Machine learning has, however, enjoyed something of a revival in the expert systems area. This is due to the fact that extracting knowledge from a domain expert is such an arduous, labour-intensive task.

In this section we will consider one much-cited machine learning algorithm in some detail and consider how this algorithm, among others, has been implemented as a tool for automatic acquisition (Hart, 1985).

7.6.1 Quinlan's ID3 algorithm

J. Ross Quinlan's Interactive Dichotomizer 3 (ID3) uses a process of induction to build a rule-based representation of the decision-making in some domain (Quinlan, 1979). To do this, the domain expert is expected to provide a set of relevant factors that influence the decision-making process. These factors are referred to as attributes. The expert is also expected to supply a set of examples of the different types of decision made. This is

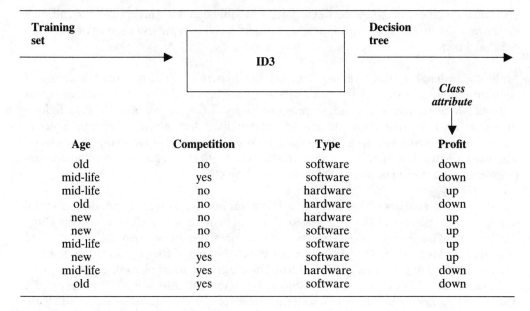

Age	Competition	Type	Profit
old	no	software	down
mid-life	yes	software	down
mid-life	no	hardware	up
old	no	hardware	down
new	no	hardware	up
new	no	software	up
mid-life	no	software	up
new	yes	software	up
mid-life	yes	hardware	down
old	yes	software	down

Figure 7.1   Set of attributes used to build a training set.

called the training set. The ID3 algorithm then uses this training set to induce general decision-making principles relevant to the domain.

Let us suppose we are given the problem of predicting whether a given company's profits will increase or decrease in the short-term future (Thompson and Thompson, 1986). Let us further suppose that we start with a simple model of three factors that affect such profits: the age of the company, whether there is any competition in the company's marketplace, and what type of company we are dealing with. We further assume that the possible values of age are *old*, *mid-life* or *new;* the possible values of type are *hardware* and *software*; and the possible values of competition are simply *yes* or *no*.

We next use this initial set of attributes to build a training set. That is, we assign a value to each attribute in turn, and then decide whether the profits of the company are likely to go up or down (see Fig. 7.1).

Quinlan's ID3 algorithm works by building a decision tree from this training set. To build a decision tree, the algorithm must select one of the attributes to be the root node of the tree. Then the algorithm must split up the training set into a number of smaller tables, each containing examples with the same value of the class attribute.

Let us suppose we select age as our starting point. The training set will then be partitioned as in Fig. 7.2. From the figure it will be seen that when age is old, profit is always down. Likewise, when age is new, profit is always up. In these two cases further partitioning is not necessary.

When age is mid-life, however, profit can either be up or down. The algorithm must therefore select a new attribute and split the training set again. Fig. 7.3 shows the result of such splitting on competition. Since each partition now contains only one value for the class attribute, the tree-building process is complete (see Fig. 7.4).

Age	Competition	Type	Profit
old	no	software	down
old	no	hardware	down
old	yes	software	down
new	no	hardware	up
new	no	software	up
new	yes	software	up
mid-life	yes	software	down
mid-life	no	hardware	up
mid-life	no	software	up
mid-life	yes	hardware	down

Figure 7.2   Training set partitioned by attribute 'age'.

Age	Competition	Type	Profit
old	no	software	down
old	no	hardware	down
old	yes	software	down
new	no	hardware	up
new	no	software	up
new	yes	software	up
mid-life	no	hardware	up
mid-life	no	software	up
mid-life	yes	hardware	down
mid-life	yes	software	down

Figure 7.3   Training set partitioned by attribute 'competition'.

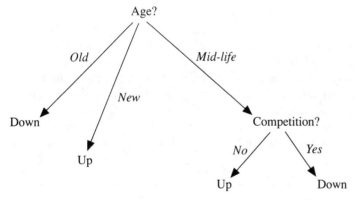

Figure 7.4   The completed decision-tree.

The decision tree we have generated is of course not the only possible tree that would describe our training set. Rather than selecting age as the root node, for instance, we might have selected competition. The question is then, how does the algorithm know which tree best represents the decision-making inherent in a particular training set?

The detail is beyond the scope of this work. Suffice it to say that the ID3 algorithm makes this decision by repeatedly partitioning the training set according to the attribute with the greatest discriminatory power; i.e. the attribute which tells us more about how to classify an object than others. Quinlan uses an information-theoretic measure of entropy – a measure of the degree of disorder in a system – for this purpose (Quinlan, 1979).

7.7 KNOWLEDGE ELICITATION AND THE PENSIONS PROJECT

In this section we illustrate the process of knowledge elicitation by considering the personal pensions project again. The question and answer sessions illustrated in Figs 7.5 to 7.10 represent condensed transcripts of a number of short interviews with the pension expert. The interviews were confined to five minutes or so at regular intervals. This was in order to fit in with the hectic schedule of the domain expert's working day.

After some analysis of transcripts, it soon became apparent that the following factors are what defined a standard case:

1. The employment status of the customer. That is, whether the customer is employed by some organization or is self-employed.
2. The likely contribution period. This is easily worked out as the number of years to age 65 for men and 60 for women.
3. Whether or not the customer is in a company pension scheme.
4. Whether or not the customer is in the state earnings-related scheme.
5. Whether the investor wants security from his pension or whether he is willing to take the risk of more venturesome investment for high gain.

7.8 CONCLUSION

In this chapter we have considered the interdependent processes of knowledge elicitation and acquisition. The aim of this chapter has been to illustrate how elicitation is the process of locating, collecting and refining the knowledge relevant to some domain. Knowledge may be collected from a number of different sources via a number of different techniques. The foremost knowledge source is still the domain expert, however, and the most prominent technique is still the face-to-face interview.

In the next chapter we discuss some related issues: how do we document the results of elicitation, and how might we use developing models to drive the process of elicitation itself?

Q: What's the end result of your present system?
A: We recommend one of a number of personal pensions to our customer.

Q: What personal pensions can you offer your customers?
A: We presently offer just three: a Prudent, Amicable or Equitable pension. For some customers we'd not recommend a pension plan as such but our own premium account.

Q: What's that?
A: It's a high interest building society account.

Figure 7.5 Question-and-answer session. Interview 1: 4.15 p.m. Friday.

Q: OK, so you offer three pension plans and one high interest building society account?
A: Yes.

Q: So let's take one of these, say an Amicable pension plan. What sort of customer would you recommend this pension plan for?
A: Well, customers who are self-employed and likely to contribute for more than ten years.

Q: Could you explain what you mean by contribute?
A: Yes. The best time to take out a pension plan is when you're in your early twenties. If you retire at 65 you will then have over 40 years of contributions.

Figure 7.6   Question-and-answer session. Interview 2: 8.55 a.m. Monday.

Q: Do you recommend Amicable for any other type of customer?
A: No.

Q: OK, so what about a Prudent pension? When would you recommend this pension plan?
A: Well, Prudent is a little more involved than Amicable. We'd recommend it in a number of cases.

Q: Could you give me an example?
A: Yes, well Prudent is normally relevant for employed persons not in company pension schemes.

Q: So let's get this right . . . somebody who's employed rather than self-employed, but not in a company pension plan would be recommended Prudent?
A: Ah, no. Only if they are in SERPS and are likely to contribute for between 10 and 22 years.

Figure 7.7.   Question-and-answer session. Interview 3: 12.55 p.m. Monday.

Q: OK, so let's go over what I've got. You'd recommend an Amicable pension to customers who are self-employed and can contribute for ten years or more?
A: Yes. That's right.

Q: You'd recommend a Prudent pension for an employed person, not in a company pension scheme, in SERPS, with a likely contribution period of between 10 and 22 years?
A: Yes. You've got it.

Figure 7.8   Question-and-answer session. Interview 4: 4.55 p.m. Monday.

Q: Can I ask you some questions about Equitable? Can you give me an example of when you would recommend an Equitable pension?
A: Well, Equitable is pretty similar to Prudent in many respects.

Q: In what way?
A: Well, we recommend it for employed persons not in company schemes but in SERPS.

Q: What distinguishes it then from a Prudent pension?
A: Well, for instance, we recommend it to people who can contribute for more than 25 years.

Q: I see. Are there any other occasions when it might look suitable?
A: Well, if people have a contribution period of between 22 and 25 years and they want high security then Equitable is the best bet.

Figure 7.9   Question-and-answer session. Interview 5: 8.55 a.m. Tuesday.

Q: We discussed Equitable last time and you mentioned high security. Could you tell me what high security means?

A: Sure. Well, first of all you must understand that all of our personal pension plans are unit trust schemes.

Q: Unit Trusts?

A: Yes. A unit trust is an investment fund in the stock market. They are designed primarily to limit the risk of investing in the stock market. Rather than purchasing a share in some company your pension contributions purchase a unit or part-unit of the unit trust fund. A fund manager then uses the collection of contributions to purchase shares on the stock market on your behalf. Most of the profits from share dealings are re-invested in the fund. Over time the capital in the fund is therefore likely to grow. It is from this accumulated fund that your pension is paid when you retire.

Q: So what does security mean in this context?

A: Although most pension funds of this nature are expected to grow, there is no guarantee of the rate at which they will grow. Some funds perform better on the stock market than others. Some poorer than others . . . The crucial point is that some funds are deliberately cautious in their investments; others not so cautious . . . Some funds are secure in the sense that their objective is moderate growth by investment in safe, long-term, performing companies. Others are willing to take more risk but with the potential for greater growth.

Figure 7.10   Question-and-answer session. Interview 6: 12.55 p.m. Tuesday.

7.9 RECALL EXERCISES

1. Are knowledge acquisition and elicitation distinct activities?
2. Describe why the classic relationship between one knowledge engineer and one domain expert is impracticable in commercial development.
3. What is the paradox of expertise?
4. List three types of knowledge source.
5. Why is cross-referencing between knowledge sources useful for knowledge engineering?
6. What sort of problems arise from distributed knowledge?
7. Describe three direct techniques.
8. What is meant by automatic knowledge acquisition?
9. Describe what you see to be some of the advantages and disadvantages of automatic acquisition.

7.10 OPEN-ENDED EXERCISES

1. The terms acquisition and elicitation tend to assume that knowledge has some form of objective existence. An alternative view of knowledge is as a subjective concept. How might this view change our conception of elicitation?
2. If knowledge is power then people will be loathe to impart knowledge. Discuss some of the social problems that might arise in knowledge elicitation.
3. Discuss whether an automatic knowledge acquisition facility can replace the knowledge engineer.

4. Discuss some of the problems that might arise in a domain where there are numerous domain experts, and experts disagree about what constitutes knowledge.

REFERENCES

Collins H.M. (1990). Knowing and growing: building an expert system for semi-conductor crystal growing. Paper presented at *Social Perspectives of Software – Oxford Workshop*, The Moathouse, 13–14 January.

Grover M.D. (1986). A pragmatic knowledge acquisition methodology. *Proceedings of the 8th International Joint Conference on Artificial Intelligence*, 436–438.

Hart A.A. (1985). The role of induction in knowledge elicitation. *Expert Systems*, **2**(1), 24–28.

Hickman F. (Ed.) (1989). *Knowledge Based Systems Analysis: A Pragmatic Introduction to the KADS Methodology*. Ellis Horwood, Cambridge.

Olson J.R. and Reuter H.H. (1987). Extracting expertise from experts: methods for knowledge acquisition. *Expert Systems*, **4**(3), 152–168.

Quinlan J.R. (1979). Discovering rules by induction from large collections of examples. In Michie D. (Ed.) *Expert Systems in the Micro-Electronic Age*. Edinburgh University Press, 168–201.

Thompson B. and Thompson W. (1986). Finding rules in data. *Byte*, November.

Wellbank M. (1983). *A Review of Knowledge Acquisition Techniques for Expert Systems*. British Telecom Research Laboratories, Martlesham Heath, Ipswich, England.

8

KNOWLEDGE ANALYSIS II: MODEL DEVELOPMENT

8.1 INTRODUCTION

In this, and the chapter that follows, we shall consider a number of distinct techniques applicable to knowledge engineering. Our aim in considering a number of different techniques throughout this work is to be as non-deterministic as possible. It is the author's belief that no one single technique offers the entire solution to the problem of documenting knowledge. We therefore discuss a toolkit of techniques designed to complement the various activities of knowledge engineering.

In this chapter we primarily discuss a number of techniques designed to act as aids to the process of knowledge elicitation. Each technique gradually builds up a model of the knowledge in some domain and encourages the use of the developing model to direct knowledge acquisition.

Many of the techniques discussed are as applicable to the design of expert systems as they are to the analysis of knowledge. We discuss them here primarily because of the way in which they have been portrayed as drivers for the knowledge elicitation process.

8.2 SPIDER DIAGRAMS

One of the major ways of conducting elicitation is via taped interviews with the domain expert. These interviews are frequently transcribed and then subjected to analysis. A complementary approach is to gradually build spider diagrams of the domain both during and subsequent to an interview.

Spider diagrams were originally devised by Tony Buzan as a more effective method of note-taking than conventional narrative text (Buzan, 1982). Their use within knowledge

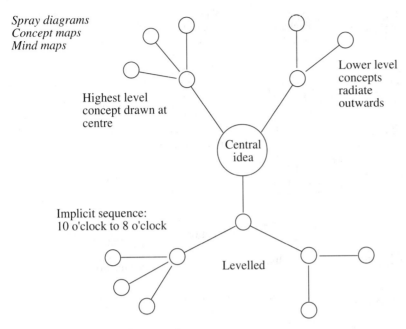

Spray diagrams
Concept maps
Mind maps

Lower level
concepts
radiate
outwards

Highest level
concept drawn at
centre

Central
idea

Implicit sequence:
10 o'clock to 8 o'clock

Levelled

Figure 8.1   Sequencing of a spider diagram.

engineering is discussed in Barrett and Beerel (1988). The idea is simply to relate concepts together in a free-form way by lines. It is conventional to start at the centre of a sheet of paper with the most important concept, or a concept which acts as a useful description of the domain. Associated concepts are then drawn radiating outwards. If sequencing is required, it is conventional to read spider diagrams from 10 o'clock around to 8 o'clock (see Fig. 8.1). Fig. 8.2 illustrates a sample spider diagram built to illustrate the relationship between concepts in the domain of knowledge engineering.

Spider diagrams can also be levelled. In other words, a concept on one diagram can act as the central source of some other diagram. In this way, spider diagrams can be used to document progressive levels of detail.

There are two ways of using spider diagrams in any interview situation (see Fig. 8.3.):

1. The knowledge engineer can radiate outwards from the central concept rather like ripples on a pond. The most direct associations are elicited first, then the next most direct, and so on.
2. The knowledge engineer can become deeply involved in a particular line of questioning before considering the next most direct concept. This means that the spider diagram grows one branch at a time.

8.3 KNOWLEDGE ANALYSIS IN KADS

In Chapter 5 we discussed how analysis in KADS is a process of developing a conceptual

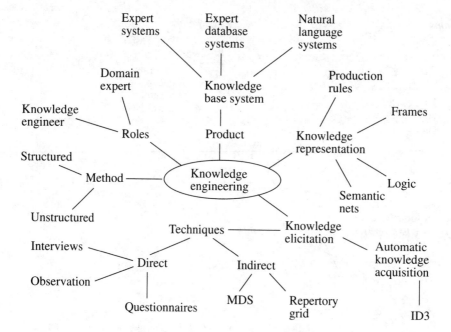

Figure 8.2 Spider diagram illustrating relationships between knowledge engineering concepts.

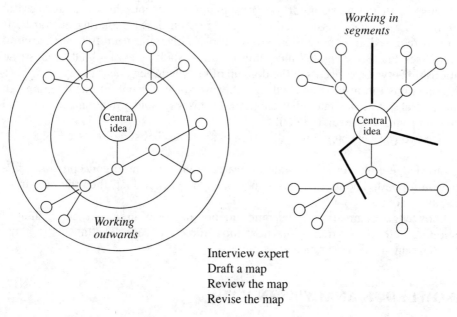

Interview expert
Draft a map
Review the map
Revise the map

Figure 8.3 Using spider diagrams in an interview.

model of some knowledge domain. This it does through the application of a so-called generic model, or composite of such models, which the knowledge engineer selects from a model library. The knowledge engineer uses the generic model to guide the elicitation process. The aim is to see to what extent the elicited material fits an existing model. The result of this exercise is a specification of the expertise in the knowledge domain. This is known in KADS as the conceptual model.

KADS maintains a particular conception of expertise which contains four layers:

1. Domain. Static knowledge describing concepts, relationships and structures.
2. Inference. Knowledge of all the different types of inferences that can be made using the static knowledge.
3. Task. Knowledge representing inferences for problem-solving tasks within the knowledge domain.
4. Strategy. Strategic knowledge for combining tasks.

The strategic layer controls the task layer by providing plans or meta-rules. The task layer applies its goals to the knowledge centred in the inference layer. The inference layer describes the application of concepts located within the domain layer.

The main characteristic of this four-layer approach is that it allows knowledge to be represented at several levels of abstraction. Only the domain layer is, by definition, domain-specific. The other layers are largely domain-independent.

The knowledge domain of fault-finding among physical devices such as computers, for instance, shares many similarities with that of medical diagnosis. Both these domains can therefore be described by roughly the same generic model. As a consequence, the layers of expertise – strategic, task and inference – can be used to define ideal–typical domains of expertise.

8.3.1 An example of the four-layer model

In this section we present a simplified example of the KADS four-layer model as applied to medical diagnosis (Hickman, 1989).

The domain layer is made up of concepts, relations and structures:

1. Concepts. Fever, spots, stomach-ache, mouth pain (symptoms); measles, gum disease, liver sclerosis (diagnosis).
2. Relations. Excessive alcohol consumption can cause liver sclerosis. Mouth pain can cause unchewed food. Unchewed food can cause stomach-ache.
3. Structures. Hierarchies of infectious diseases. Causal networks of diseases.

The inference layer uses one of the library of generic models to relate so-called meta-classes (see Fig. 8.4). This model maintains four such meta-classes:

1. Observables, e.g. temperature of 41 degrees C; diastolic blood pressure of 110 mmHg.
2. Evidence, e.g. high fever; hypertension.
3. Hypotheses, e.g. bacterial infection; nefral problem.
4. Solutions, e.g. pneumonia caused by pneumococcera.

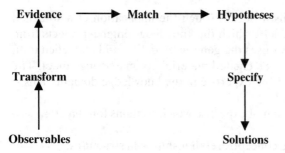

Figure 8.4   Relation of meta-classes using a generic model.

Each meta-class is processed via one of three processes *transform*, *match* and *specify*. The transform process can be implemented as an abstraction mechanism that applies qualitative definitions to observables. Matching can be supported by a series of heuristics. Finally, specification can be carried out by a specialization mechanism.

The task layer will specify whether the domain is data-driven or goal-driven. In a data-driven approach we start with observables and move forward to solutions. In a goal-driven approach we hypothesize a particular solution and then look for evidence to support it.

The strategy layer will be concerned with determining the choice of the task structure and the level of refinement of the system. The cost of obtaining data is the major factor in determining the choice between a goal-driven and data-driven task structure. If, for instance, the cost of obtaining data is high then a goal-driven approach will be more appropriate.

Sometimes, specifying a detailed solution to a problem is unnecessary. In an emergency situation, for instance, it may be more important to get an approximate diagnosis quickly so that treatment can be administered. In this case the level of refinement of the proposed system can be low.

8.4 NORMALIZING KNOWLEDGE

Debenham (1985) has proposed that a technique conventionally applied to the design of database systems be adapted to the exigencies of knowledge base development. This technique, known variously as determinacy or dependency diagramming, is used normally to document the association between data-items as a preliminary step to producing a normalized database. Normalization is the process of producing a redundancy-free design for database. Debenham has illustrated how the technique may be applied to what he calls knowledge chunks. He maintains that this technique offers the following advantages (Debenham, 1985, 1987):

1. It offers a rigorous method for systematically acquiring all the knowledge relevant to a particular domain.
2. The method encourages the simplification of knowledge.
3. The technique refines knowledge. That is, it ensures that individual chunks of knowledge do not overlap.

4. It offers the ability to establish the internal consistency of a model representing the knowledge domain.

We illustrate the technique here with an example adapted from Debenham (1985). Suppose our knowledge engineer has elicited the following description of the knowledge domain. We describe the knowledge via a series of assertions:

1. All people at Cymro are called employees.
2. Each employee is identified by a unique employee number.
3. Employees are divided into three classes: divisional managers are class 1; branch managers are class 2; all other employees are class 3.
4. All employees, except divisional managers, are assigned to a unique branch, identified by a branch number.
5. Each branch is assigned one branch manager.
6. Each employee is assigned a unique supervisor.
7. Employees are supervised by the manager of the branch in which they work.
8. Each branch manager is supervised by one divisional manager.

Each assertion can be represented on a dependency diagram. Assertion 3 can be represented by the diagram in Fig. 8.5a. This dependency or determinancy diagram essentially asserts that the information contained in *EmpClass* can be deduced from the information contained in *EmpJob*. *EmpClass* and *EmpJob* are said to be part of a functional dependency. For every value of *EmpJob* there is only one value of *EmpClass* associated with it.

A number of other functional dependencies can be identified from the assertions. Assertion 4 can be represented by Fig. 8.5b, and assertion 5 is represented by Fig. 8.5c.

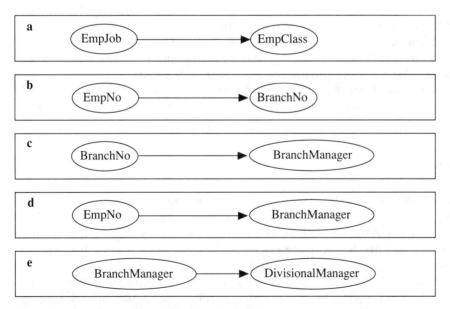

Figure 8.5   Assertions represented as dependency diagrams.

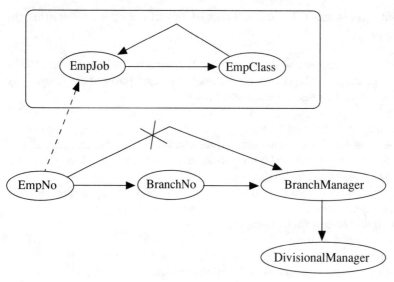

Figure 8.6 Plotting of assertions discovered in domain.

Assertions 6 and 7 can be represented by Fig. 8.5d, while assertion 8 is documented in Fig. 8.5e.

Debenham emphasizes using this technique as a means of driving knowledge elicitation. Hence, we would be plotting all the assertions discovered of a domain in a diagram as in Fig. 8.6. We would then ask questions directly of this model. For instance:

1. There is clearly a functional dependency in both directions between *EmpJob* and *EmpClass*. *EmpJob* and *EmpClass* are therefore theoretically equivalent. The question therefore arises: is there a need for both these items in our model?
2. No association between *EmpNo* and *EmpJob* is indicated in the assertions above. This, however, would seem a sensible way of connecting two separate clumps of determinancy. We therefore confirm this with the domain expert.
3. We have a so-called transitive dependency between *EmpNo*, *BranchNo* and *Branch-Manager*. Can we therefore remove the direct link between *EmpNo* and *BranchMa-nager*?

8.5 NIAM

Debenham sees dependency diagramming as a step towards the exploitation of a full information analysis method within knowledge engineering. In this light, NIAM (Njissen's Information Analysis Method), a method originally designed for documenting information requirements, has been seen as useful by many in the knowledge engineering community (Verheijen and Van Bekkum, 1982).

The major part of NIAM is the conceptual grammar. The conceptual grammar is a technique for formally specifying the knowledge contained in the natural language descriptions of some domain.

The conceptual grammar makes the distinction between lexical and non-lexical objects. Lexical objects (LOTS) are strings that can be uttered and which refer to an object. Examples are surnames, street names and town names. Non-lexical objects (NOLOTS) are real or abstract things which are not utterable. Examples are persons, streets and towns. LOTS are fundamentally what we described as being objects in Chapter 3. NOLOTS are classes of objects.

A simple natural language sentence such as:

Jones has an account at Pontypridd Branch

can be transformed into a structure composed of LOTS and NOLOTS:

The person with the surname Jones
has an account at
the branch with the branch name Pontypridd

In fact, sentences of this type can be classified as follows:

a person referred to by surname
has an account at
a branch referred to by branch name

This form of structure specifies the association between NOLOTS or the association between LOTS and NOLOTS. The association between NOLOTS is referred to as an instance of an idea type. The association between a LOT and a NOLOT is referred to as an instance of a bridge type. The sentence, *person lives in town* is an instance of an idea type. The sentence, *person is referred to by surname* is an example of a bridge type.

NIAM uses a graphic notation to specify conceptual structures of this form. Fig. 8.7 illustrates the basic constructs of NIAM notation.

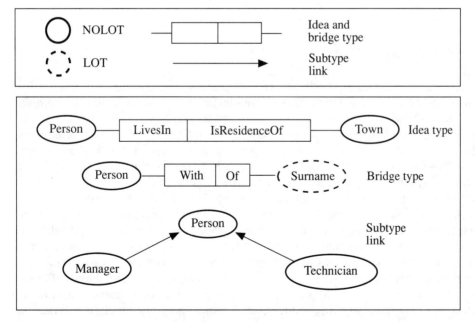

Figure 8.7   Basic constructs of NIAM notation.

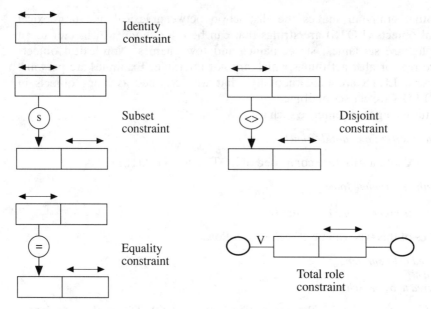

Figure 8.8 Constraint types of NIAM.

One of the most interesting things about NIAM is its ability to attach a range of constraints to the conceptual grammar. This makes it an excellent vehicle for detailed knowledge description, and complements other information analysis techniques such as extended E–R diagramming which we shall consider in the next chapter. Figure 8.8 illustrates the constraint types of NIAM.

8.6 CONCEPTUAL GRAPHS

NIAM has been much used both as an information engineering and knowledge engineering method on the Continent. A related technique known as *conceptual graphs* has had more influence in the United States. Conceptual graphs are a powerful technique for representing knowledge based on the work on semantic nets in cognitive psychology and AI (Sowa, 1984). They can be used to represent the propositions of first-order logic as well as those of the higher logics. One of the advantages of this technique is that it encourages a clear hierarchical organization of knowledge.

The basic concepts of a conceptual graph can be illustrated with a simple example. The graph in Fig. 8.9a represents the sentence 'the customer is making the claim'. There are three fundamental elements displayed in this graph: concepts, conceptual relations and directed arcs. Concepts represent the primitives of knowledge relevant to some domain. Conceptual relations and their directed arcs define the various roles concepts play in defining other concepts. Conceptual relations are represented by labelled ellipses. Directed arcs link relations to concepts. Concepts are prohibited from being directly linked to other concepts. Similarly, conceptual relations may not be directly linked to other relations.

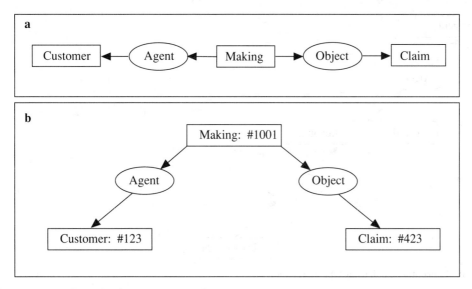

Figure 8.9   Example of a conceptual graph.

The concepts represented in Fig. 8.9a are known as *generic* concepts. In such concepts no particular individual is being referenced. To refer to the extension of concepts a referent field and marker are added to the basic notation. Each specific object in a universe of discourse is given a unique reference marker (a # followed by a unique number, or some unique name). Fig. 8.9b represents a graph detailing the fact that a specific customer (#123) and a specific insurance claim (#423) is taking place in a specific claim-making event (#1001).

The full conceptual graph language proposed by Sowa includes constructs for a vast array of knowledge structures:

1. Type definitions. A concept may be defined in terms of necessary and sufficient conditions.
2. Prototypes. A prototype represents the typical features or default information associated with the definition of some object.
3. Schemas. The later Wittgenstein made the observation that it is not always possible to give intensional definitions of concepts. For example, the only real way we can understand the concept of a game is by being aware of the different ways in which we use the concept of a game. In this sense, the concept of a game is made up of a set of schema (conceptual graphs) each representing a different aspect of the concept.
4. Individuals. In the language of conceptual graphs an individual is a graph which represents the aggregate of all the associated information stored about an individual.
5. Canonical graphs. The conceptual graph language needs a mechanism for disallowing such spurious concepts as those embodied in the perfectly grammatical sentence: 'green ideas sleep furiously'. To rule out this possibility we would need to ensure that there is no canonical graph which had IDEA as an agent of the concept of sleep.
6. Propositions. This is a graphic representation of rules and rule-sets.

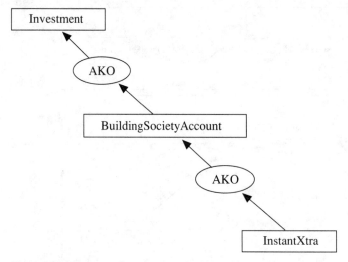

Figure 8.10 Conceptual graph using type hierarchies.

Conceptual graphs may be represented in a more tractable linear form. The graph in Fig. 8.9a would be represented by the following notation:

[customer: #123]←(agent)←[making: #1001]→(object)→[claim: #423]

Conceptual graphs can also incorporate generalization through the use of type hierarchies. The conceptual relations ISA and AKO can be used to connect instances to classes and subclasses to super-classes as indicated in Chapter 3. Hence, the graph:

[investment]←(ako)←[building society account]←(ako)←[Instant Xtra]

would represent the fact that building society accounts are a type of investment. This is illustrated as a graph in Fig. 8.10.

8.7 DRIVING PENSION ACQUISITION

Figure 8.11 illustrates a first-stage spider diagram for the pension project. The diagram has been built up from the interview transcripts presented in Chapter 7. Note how we have built up the diagram in segments. This follows the line of enquiry conducted by the knowledge engineer in which she derived deep information on each type of recommendation in turn.

Figure 8.12 documents the associations between data-items in the pension domain as a determinancy diagram. This knowledge would have been gained by both an analysis of previous information forms and interviews with the domain expert. Note that we have chosen to give each new customer a serial number called *Customer No;* this determines most of the data-items of relevance to selecting pensions. Note, however, how the critical group of items – *CompanyScheme, Security, Serps, ContributionPeriod* and *EmploymentStatus* – in themselves determine a given pension recommendation.

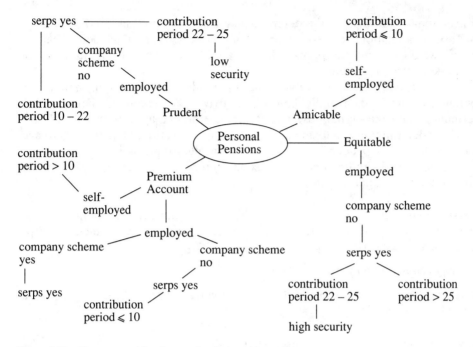

Figure 8.11   First-stage spider diagram for the pensions project.

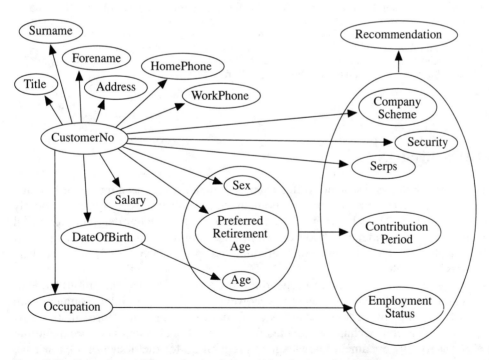

Figure 8.12   Determinancy diagram showing the associations between data-items.

In conventional data analysis the determinancy diagram would be used to design a database, usually a relational database (see Beynon-Davies, 1992). Each determinant in the diagram would become the primary key of a table. Dependent data-items would become non-key attributes of tables.

As it stands we would need five tables: one for standard customer information, one representing what are fundamentally the rules for arriving at a recommendation, a table for determining contribution periods, a table for determining ages from dates of birth and a table for determining employment_status from occupation. Date of birth to age, however, is clearly a dependency best suited to an algorithm, as is the dependency between age, preferred_retirement_age, sex and contribution_period. This leaves us with three tables defined below:

Customers(*customer no*, sname, fname, address, marital_status, home_phone, work_phone, dob, occupation, salary, sex, preferred_retirement, serps, company_scheme, security)

Occupations(*occupation*, employment_status)

Rules(*rule no*, serps, employment_status, company_scheme, security, contribution_period, recommendation)

Note how we introduce a surrogate identifier to identify rules.

Fig. 8.13 illustrates a simple analysis of the pension domain conducted using the conceptual grammar of NIAM. The diagram documents the following knowledge:

> Applicants for personal pensions are either existing customers or new customers. New and existing customers can be identified by a combination of surname and forename. Customers fill in customer information forms. Each information form is for one customer but a customer can fill in a number of forms. Existing customers hold building society accounts. A building society account is identified by an account number. Each account is held by only one customer, but a customer can hold a number of different accounts.

8.8 CONCLUSION

Each of the techniques discussed in this chapter is meant to act as a means of building conceptual models of some knowledge domain. Spider diagrams are useful in loosely documenting relationships between elicited concepts. Determinancy diagrams are useful in documenting dependencies between knowledge chunks. An information analysis method such as NIAM's conceptual grammar is particularly useful in specifying constraints.

All of the techniques are used to drive the process of knowledge elicitation. None of the techniques are sufficient by themselves, however, to allow us to fully document both the declarative and procedural knowledge of some domain. Therefore, in the next chapter we look at four techniques adapted from conventional systems development that will allow us to fully document knowledge in preparation for the design of a knowledge base system.

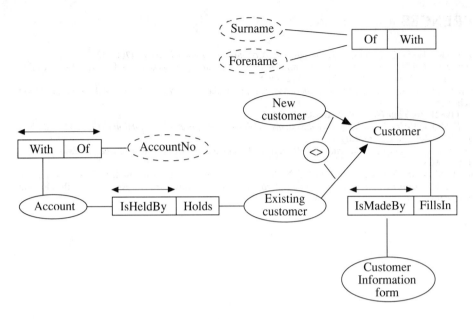

Figure 8.13 Analysis of pensions domain using NIAM.

8.9 RECALL EXERCISES

1. What is a spider diagram?
2. Why is a spider diagram better than an interview transcript as a document of knowledge?
3. Describe two ways of developing spider diagrams?
4. What is meant by the conceptual grammar in NIAM?
5. What is a determinancy diagram?
6. What is a functional dependency?
7. In what way are determinancy diagrams useful for knowledge engineering?
8. What is meant by a generic model in the context of KADS?
9. What is the four-layer model of KADS?

8.10 OPEN-ENDED EXERCISES

1. Discuss the advantage of applying a technique such as NIAM to documenting knowledge as opposed to narrative text.
2. Compare and contrast NIAM and conceptual graphs as tools for model development.
3. Discuss some of the advantages of normalizing knowledge.
4. Express the knowledge documented in Fig. 8.13 as a conceptual graph.

REFERENCES

Debenham J.K. (1985). Knowledge base design. *The Australian Computer Journal*, **17**(1), 42–48.

Debenham J.K. (1987). Expert systems: an information processing perspective. In J. Ross Quinlan (Ed.) *Applications of Expert Systems*. Addison-Wesley, Sydney.

Barrett M.L. and Beerel A.C. (1988). *Expert Systems in Business: A Practical Approach*. Ellis Horwood, Chichester.

Buzan A. (1982) *Use Your Head*. BBC Books, London.

Hickman F. (Ed.) (1989). *Knowledge Based Systems Analysis: A Pragmatic Introduction to the KADS Methodology*. Ellis Horwood, Cambridge.

Sowa J.F. (1984). *Conceptual Structures: Information Processing in Mind and Machine*. Addison-Wesley, Reading, MA.

Verheijen G.M.A. and Van Bekkum J. (1982) NIAM: an information analysis method. In Olle T.W. and Sol H.G. (Eds.) *Information Systems Design Methodologies: A Comparative Review*. North Holland, Amsterdam.

DOCUMENTING KNOWLEDGE: MOVING FROM ANALYSIS TO DESIGN

9.1 INTRODUCTION

In Chapter 7 we defined knowledge elicitation as being the process of locating, collecting and refining the knowledge relevant to a particular domain. In much of the literature, the end result of the knowledge elicitation process is usually held to be a completed knowledge base expressed probably in terms of some rule set which represents the knowledge in a particular domain. Chapter 5 made the point, however, that a large rule set is not a satisfactory mechanism for representing the first results of the knowledge elicitation process. We really need, therefore, some more appropriate means for representing knowledge, means that we can present to and discuss with the user prior to implementing the first prototype. Some mechanisms for doing this will form the basis of this chapter. We do not claim that the techniques discussed form an exhaustive set. We merely claim that they are especially useful in illustrating how conventional systems development techniques can be adapted to the needs of knowledge engineering (Swaffield and Knight, 1990).

9.2 DATA-FLOW DIAGRAMS AND ENTITY–RELATIONSHIP DIAGRAMS

The two major notations of traditional structured systems analysis and design are *data-flow diagrams* (DFDs for short) and *entity–relationship diagrams* (E–R diagrams for short). These two techniques have traditionally been used to document in diagrammatic form the two major ways in which any information system may be considered: in dynamic terms, or in static terms. Viewing an information system dynamically involves documenting the way in which information flows through the system and is transformed by the various processes which make up the system. Viewing a system statically involves detailing the structure of the information needed to support the activities of a given information system. Both such techniques have been found useful in traditional software development for a number of reasons:

1. They are relatively easy to understand by people not versed in the intricacies of systems analysis and design.
2. They emphasize the importance of data rather than process. That is, the prime area of concern is the data needed to support organizational behaviour. The processes undertaken in any organization are seen to be by-products of, or reliant upon, organizational data. This viewpoint encourages a global, integrated structure for the data of an enterprise.
3. They emphasize the importance of conceptual modelling. That is, the desirability of building an initial, abstract model of the system which is not tied to any specific implementation plan.

In an earlier chapter we made the point that a knowledge base system is a logical extension of the database concept. Both E–R diagrams and DFDs have been found invaluable in the process of designing traditional database systems. It is only a small step to consider how they might be used, and perhaps extended, to encompass the analysis and design of knowledge base systems.

Most of the benefits of DFDs and E–R diagrams carry over into the knowledge engineering arena:

1. A picture presented to a domain expert is worth a thousand rules. The average domain expert is unlikely to understand the intricacies of a knowledge base using the production rule formalism, for instance. Presenting the domain expert with a large number of rules is therefore unlikely to elicit much favourable response. Presenting the domain expert with a picture based in a powerful notation is, however, another matter. Such a diagram is much more likely to be understood in practical terms and hence responded to.
2. It may be more beneficial to concentrate initially on knowledge rather than the complexities of inference. The various inferencing techniques employed, such as backward and forward chaining, usually arise naturally from a detailed discussion of the concepts and relationships relevant to a domain.
3. As we discussed in Chapter 5, there are inherent dangers in the unbridled application of the rapid prototyping technique much favoured in knowledge engineering. The major danger is that the developed prototype might begin to constitute a hotchpotch of ill-considered rules and facts. In contrast, the purpose of the techniques to be discussed is to force the knowledge engineer to be more considerate, in the sense that he takes time to agree an initial specification for the knowledge to be modelled by the system. The end result of this is that the knowledge base is much more likely to form an ordered, well-structured entity.

As well as the reasons presented above there is another major benefit arising from the application of traditional structured systems analysis techniques to knowledge engineering. That is, they encourage the production of knowledge base systems that are embedded within, or which interact with, conventional software systems. This is extremely important if knowledge engineering is to become a substantial commercial proposition.

9.3 ENTITY–RELATIONSHIP DIAGRAMMING

Addis (1987) has used a specialized form of entity–relationship diagramming for the analysis and design of knowledge base systems. We discuss here a more conventional approach to E–R diagramming and some extensions which make it particularly applicable to knowledge engineering.

An E–R diagram is a model of an information system in terms of entities, and the relationships between such entities.

An entity may be defined as 'a thing which the enterprise recognizes as being capable of an independent existence and which can be uniquely identified' (Howe, 1983).

In information terms such characteristics normally define a 'data group'; that is, a group of data-items associated with a particular entity. Imagine, for instance, a basic personnel system as used by Cymro. Typically there might be a number of entities in this environment which we could readily define: StaffMember, Branch, Customer, Pension, etc.

Each of these entities could be described by a group of attributes. For instance, StaffMember might have the attributes: staffNumber, name, address, numberOfYears Service, etc.

A relationship can be defined as 'an association between two or more entities' (Beynon-Davies, 1992). An important relationship in the personnel application might be 'employs' – a Branch employs StaffMembers.

An entity is represented on a diagram by a rectangular box in which is written a meaningful name for the entity (Fig. 9.1a). A relationship between two entities is represented by drawing a labelled line between the relevant boxes (Fig. 9.1b).

There are a number of properties of the concept of relationship which are usually considered important, the most important of which is the degree of a relationship. A relationship can be said to be either a 1:1 (one-to-one) relationship, a 1:M (one-to-many) relationship, or a M:N (many-to-many) relationship.

For instance, the relationship between staff and customers can be said to be one-to-one (1:1) if it can be defined in the following way:

A StaffMember services at most one Customer.
A Customer may be serviced by, at most, one StaffMember.

In contrast, the relationship between staff and customers is one-to-many (1:M) if it is defined as:

A StaffMember services many Customers.
A Customer may be serviced by at most one StaffMember.

Finally, we are approaching a realistic representation of the relationship when we describe it as being many-to-many (M:N). That is:

a Entities

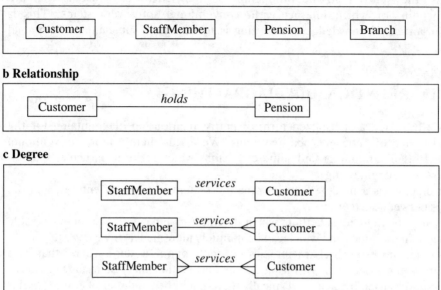

b Relationship

c Degree

Figure 9.1 Representation of entities, relationships and degree of relationships.

A StaffMember services many Customers.
A Customer may be serviced by many StaffMembers.

There are a number of competing notational devices available for portraying the degree of a relationship. We choose to represent degree by drawing a crow's foot on the many end of a relationship (Fig. 9.1c).

9.3.1 Extensions to entity–relationship diagramming

Entity–relationship diagramming has undoubtedly become one of the pre-eminent analysis and design techniques in the database area. Created in the mid-1970s, the technique has been the subject of numerous conferences and research papers. As a result, the original data model as proposed by P.P.S. Chen has been extended in a number of directions (Chen, 1976). The overall intention of these extensions has been to provide a consistent approach to modelling aspects of the real world which were not well handled by the original data model (Beynon-Davies, 1992). Perhaps the foremost of these extensions are the so-called abstraction mechanisms.

A number of abstraction mechanisms have been proposed for database design. Three fundamental abstraction mechanisms have been found important for such work: generalization, aggregation and association.

Perhaps the most popular abstraction mechanism is that of generalization. Generalization is the process by which a higher-order entity is formed by emphasizing the similarities between a number of lower-level entities. An *Employee* entity, for instance, might be considered a generalization of *Manager, StaffMember, Technician*, etc. A

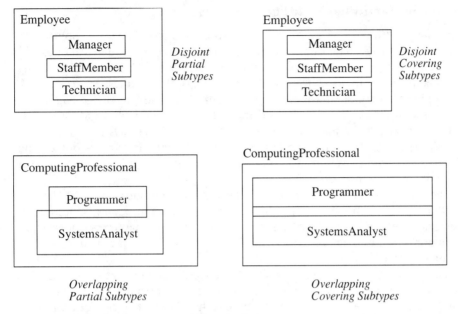

Figure 9.2 Generalization represented by nesting boxes.

ComputingProfessional entity might likewise be considered a generalization of *SystemsAnalyst*, *Programmer*, *DatabaseAdministrator*, etc. One way of indicating generalization is by nesting lower-order entity boxes within higher-order entity boxes. Higher-order entities are frequently referred to as classes, while lower-order entities are referred to as subclasses or subtypes (see Fig. 9.2).

It is useful to make a distinction between partial and covering subtypes of an entity. If subtypes are partial then other subtypes can be included. If subtypes are covering, then no further subtypes are permitted. Hence, if we regard *Manager*, *Secretary* and *Technician* as partial subtypes of *Employee* then other subtypes such as *ShopFloorWorker* are possible. If these subtypes are covering, then *Manager*, *Secretary* and *Technician* are the only types of *Employee* we can have in our company.

The lower-order entities in the two examples given above probably do not overlap. A *Manager* cannot be a *Secretary* or a *Technician* and a *Book* cannot be a *Journal* or a *Magazine*. We can conceive of real-world situations, however, where the concepts embodied in entity types do overlap. Hence we might define two types of *Computing Professional*, *SystemsAnalyst* and *Programmer*, which in many firms frequently do overlap. In such cases we draw overlapping boxes (see Fig. 9.2).

Aggregation and association can also be represented on E–R diagrams. Aggregation is the process by which a higher-level object is used to group together a number of lower-level objects. For instance, *iSBN*, *title*, *author*, *publisher* and *dateOfPublication* may all be aggregated together to form a book entity. In the E–R model, therefore, aggregation is implicit in assigning attributes to an entity. Association is a form of abstraction in which instances of one object are associated with instances of another object. Association is, of course, implicit in the way we define relationships on E–R diagrams.

9.3.2 Application of entity models to knowledge engineering

Entities are simply 'things' of interest in the studied environment or domain. In traditional information system terms, such 'things' normally represent items about which information is needed to be stored. It is necessary to describe the properties of the thing, and there is a need to indicate to which other things the entities are related. In knowledge engineering the emphasis is not wholly different. The knowledge engineer in his first interviews with the domain expert is trying to identify roughly what 'things' the expert feels are important, in terms of how he performs his function, or what goes into making up his expertise. These things might be called concepts, factors, or objects, but they still represent elements that will probably be used in the knowledge base as component parts of rules and facts.

For instance, in our expert system for selecting personal pensions, we might find the following 'things' to be important in this knowledge domain: contributionPeriod, employmentStatus, etc. Each of these 'things' constitutes factors that the pensions expert sees to be important in making a recommendation of a personal pension. In this sense, the entity or object of interest is a customer. Each of the above factors constitute attributes that can be used to describe this object. Further, each of the attributes can take on one of a number of possible values in any particular case. Any one property can hence be described in terms of a series of object–attribute–value (OAV) triples. For example:

> PBD contributionPeriod 34
> PBD employmentStatus self–employed

Such triples form the usual component elements of production rules. For example, the following rule might exist in a knowledge base for the pension expert system:

> IF employmentStatus is self–employed
> and contributionPeriod$\geqslant$ 10
> Then recommendation is amicable

Entity–relationship diagrams are therefore useful for knowledge engineering in that they help to identify and relate the various elements – objects, attributes and values – that will eventually be manipulated in any knowledge base. A related approach to that discussed in this section is proposed by Finkelstein (1989).

9.4 OBJECT DICTIONARIES

When the structure of the knowledge in the domain becomes detailed, documentation via E–R diagrams becomes overly cumbersome. In such situations the knowledge is more conveniently represented in the form of a data dictionary. A data dictionary is conventionally defined as a central repository for all the meta-data relevant to a particular application. We shall extend the mechanism to represent all the objects in a particular domain. We shall therefore refer to this extended mechanism as an *object dictionary*.

We use a modified version of Backus-Naur form to make entries in our object dictionary. Backus-Naur form is a meta-language, originally designed as a means for

---

Modified Backus–Naur Form – a meta-language

$=$	item to left consists of whatever is to right
$+$	equivalent to 'and'
$[\,.\,.\,]$	selection
$\{\,.\,.\,\}$	iteration
$(\,.\,.\,)$	operational
$*\,.\,.\,*$	comment
$\wedge\,.\,.\,\wedge$	AKO – inheritance link

Figure 9.3 Notation used in Backus-Naur form.

specifying the syntax of programming languages. Fig. 9.3 illustrates the notation used. The notation can easily be used to specify the generalization relationships between objects via the AKO or inheritance link.

We will also normally append the string *unknown* to selections of this type and indicate the default that applies in this case. We give a small example in the definition below:

```
Investment = investmentNo + startDate + {debit} + {credit}
BuildingSocietyAccount = ^Investment^ + currentBalance
Customer = customerName + customerAddress + customerTel–no + {Investment}
credit = date + amount
debit = date + amount
```

9.5 DOCUMENTING PROCEDURAL KNOWLEDGE

In Chapter 5 we made the point that a large prototypical rule set is not a satisfactory mechanism for representing the products of the first results of the knowledge elicitation process. More appropriate means are needed for initially representing knowledge: means which we can present to and discuss with the user prior to implementing the first prototype.

In the previous section, we discussed the appropriateness of one particular mechanism taken from traditional software development, namely entity–relationship diagramming, for knowledge engineering. An extended version of E–R diagramming is really a means for representing the declarative knowledge in a domain; that is, detail about the type of 'things' that will form the component elements of facts in our knowledge base.

This section discusses an associated technique from structured systems analysis and design, namely data-flow diagramming. This is a technique which can be used for representing procedural knowledge; that is, information about how elements represented in a set of extended E–R diagrams are manipulated within the expertise of the domain.

9.6 DATA-FLOW DIAGRAMMING

A data-flow diagram (DFD) is a representation of a system or subsystem in terms of how data or information moves through the system.

A number of people have been involved in developing the data-flow diagram as an analysis and design tool. Among the earliest exponents of the method were Tom De-Marco and Edward Yourdon (De-Marco, 1979). Gane and Sarson have modified and extended the technique to approach something like the technique discussed in this chapter (Gane and Sarson, 1977). The major difference of this technique is in the notation. We shall be using the notation recommended within the British methodology SSADM (Structured Systems Analysis and Design Methodology) (Cutts, 1991).

Probably the easiest way to understand the rationale behind a data-flow diagram is to make the analogy between an information system and a household plumbing system. Plumbing systems are designed to handle flows of water. Information systems are designed to handle flows of data. A plumbing system receives its water from external sources such as the public water supply, and deposits its used water in external entities such as drains. An information system receives its data from external sources such as customers, banks, retailers, etc., and communicates the results of its processing to other entities, perhaps other information systems. Household plumbing systems are usually designed to process water in some way. For instance, a boiler engages in the process of heating the water to a given temperature. In information systems, far more various forms of processing occur; data is transformed by some process and then passed on to another process, and so on. Finally, in a plumbing system there are usually repositories of water, e.g. sinks, cisterns, etc. In information systems, such repositories are referred to as data stores.

Data-flow diagrams are hence made up of four basic elements:

1. Processes.
2. Data flows.
3. Data stores.
4. External entities (sometimes called sources or sinks).

A process is a transformation of incoming data flow(s) into outgoing flow(s). A process is represented on a DFD by a labelled square or rectangle as in Fig. 9.4c.

A data flow is a pipeline through which packets of information of known composition flow. Data flow is represented on a DFD by a labelled directed arrow as in Fig. 9.4b.

A data store is a repository of data. For example, a waste-paper basket, a register, a card index, an indexed-sequential file on tape. A data store is represented on a DFD by an open rectangle or box with an appropriate label as in Fig. 9.4d.

An external entity (also called a source or sink) is some thing (usually a person, department or organization) lying outside the context of the system, that is a net originator or receiver of system data. An external entity is represented on a DFD by

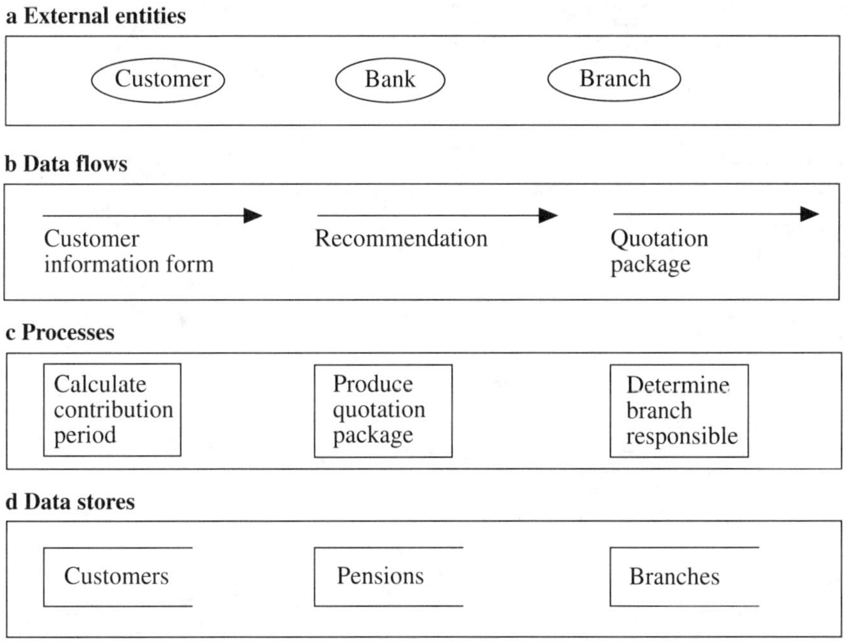

a External entities

Customer   Bank   Branch

b Data flows

Customer
information form   Recommendation   Quotation
package

c Processes

| Calculate contribution period | Produce quotation package | Determine branch responsible |

d Data stores

| Customers | Pensions | Branches |

Figure 9.4   Data-flow diagram constructs.

some form of rounded shape – a circle, an oval or a lozenge – with an appropriate name, as in Fig. 9.4a. Note that entities on DFDs should not be confused with entities on E–R diagrams.

9.6.1 Levelling

Most real-life systems are too involved to represent as a DFD on one single sheet of paper. In representing systems, systems analysts therefore usually approach the problem in a top-down manner. They attempt to level the problem beginning with an overview diagram of the entire system. As a minimum this might be made up of one process with associated flows, stores and entities. They then take the process or processes represented on the overview DFD and break them down into their own DFDs. They may continue this decomposition process for a number of levels until they can represent the entire system in sufficient detail.

Given that our system of DFDs represents a hierarchically organized documentation system, a number of conventions are normally applied to the construction of such a system (see Fig. 9.5).

First, each DFD is headed with the name of its parent process. In the case of the overview diagram this will of course represent the title of the system. For all other DFDs it will refer to the master process which is exploded in the present DFD.

Second, all inputs and outputs between parent and child diagrams are balanced. If flows A and B input to process 1 and flow C outputs, then the child diagram should also detail flows A, B and C.

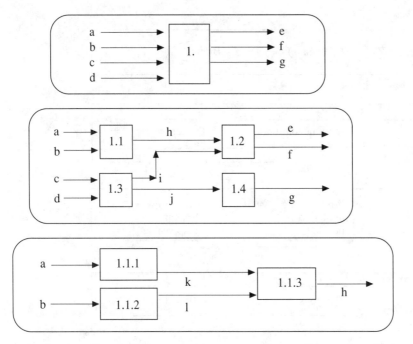

Figure 9.5   Levelling of a DFD.

Third, to indicate the position in the DFD hierarchy of any particular process, it is found useful to number uniquely each process within a documentation system.

9.6.2 Application of DFDs to knowledge engineering

The question remains, however, how do we interpret the symbols on our DFD, particularly in terms of an expert system?

Each process box on the DFD represents an independent subsystem. Each such subsystem is traditionally described in more detail by a mini-spec – a representation in a specification language, such as Structured English, of the function or activities of a particular process (Beynon-Davies, 1989). In terms of a rule-based system, such a specification might constitute a set of applicable rules (Keller, 1987).

In contrast, each data flow represents a concrete piece of knowledge used in the domain. The structure of such knowledge might be represented by a set of E–R diagrams as discussed in Section 9.3.

If the processes on our DFD represent rule sets, there still remains the question of how such rule sets are inferenced. If we are using some expert system shell or other such development tool, the inferencing mechanism will be a global one. In other words, each of the subsystems will be handled in a similar manner by the inference engine. All we need to concern ourselves with is the knowledge needed to represent each of the subsystems.

If, however, there is a need to implement the expert system in a lower-level representation, perhaps even in some traditional procedural language, each such

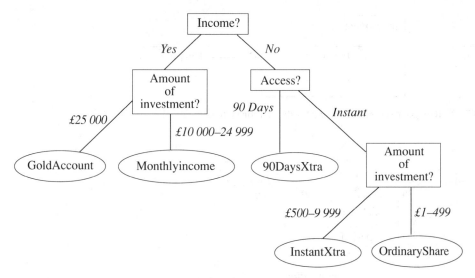

Figure 9.6   Simple decision tree used by Cymro to distinguish different accounts.

subsystem will probably need to have an inference mechanism written specifically for it. In this case, we would use data-flow diagrams in two distinct ways: first, to represent the partitioning of the overall system into subsystems; and second, to represent the inferencing processes needed to support the knowledge base.

9.7 DECISION TREES

Most of the processes included on the DFDs representing knowledge base systems involve multiple nested conditions. Decision trees are a useful mechanism for representing such processes. A decision tree is a tree in which the nodes are questions and the arcs represent the answers to questions. The terminal nodes of the tree represent conclusions. Figure 9.6 represents a simple decision tree used at Cymro to distinguish between different building society accounts.

9.8 DOCUMENTING KNOWLEDGE IN THE PENSIONS PROJECT

In this section we illustrate the application of the techniques discussed to the personal pensions project. Our aim is to document the procedural and declarative knowledge of the pensions domain.

We first set the context for the system by drawing an extended E–R diagram as in Fig. 9.7. Personal pensions are only one of a number of investments marketed by branches of Cymro to their customers. We shall discuss other investment types in Chapter 11 and 12.

Fig. 9.8 represents a simple overview DFD for the pension system. We first calculate

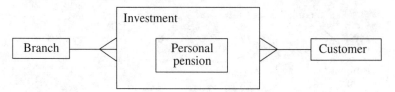

Figure 9.7   E–R diagram setting the context for the pension system.

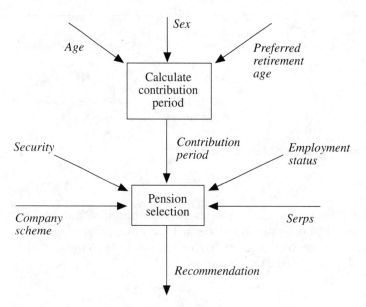

Figure 9.8   Overview DFD for the pension system.

the contribution period relevant to a particular customer. Then we use this result along with other factors to determine an appropriate recommendation for the customer.

Each process box on this DFD can be further documented as a decision tree. Figure 9.9 illustrates an attempt at diagramming the connections between the various factors in the pension selection process.

To complete our documentation we need a decision tree for the calculate contribution period process. Figure 9.10 illustrates how we might represent this, including how we might handle appropriate error-checking.

DFDs and decision trees are, however, insufficient mechanisms to fully document all the knowledge in the pension domain. We also need some mechanism of documenting our framework for facts. Figure 9.11 illustrates how we might build up an object dictionary from information provided in our DFD and decision trees. Note how we add appropriate defaults and validation mechanisms to our system. Note also how we make a distinction in the dictionary between the contribution calculated for a customer and the contribution bands relevant to the system. The object dictionary also includes suitable error-checking which has been transposed onto the decision tree.

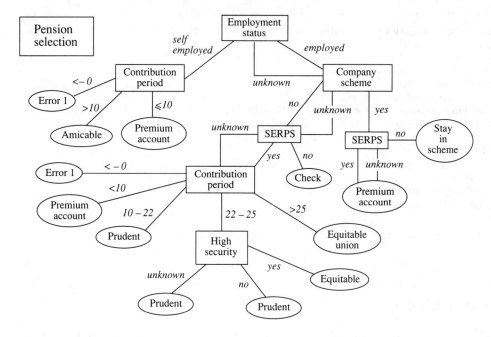

Figure 9.9   Decision tree illustrating connections between factors in the pension selection process.

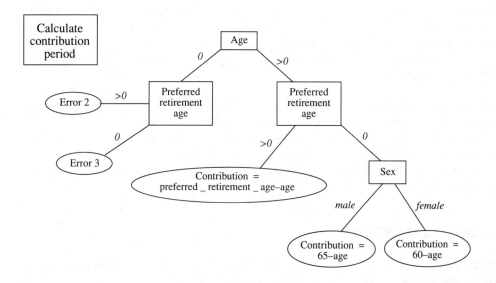

Figure 9.10   Decision tree for the calculate contribution period process.

recommendation = [prudent; amicable; equitable; (default) premium_account;
stay_in_scheme; check]
employment_status = [self_employed; (default) employed]
company_scheme = [yes; (default) no]
serps = [yes; (default) no]
security = [high; (default) low; unknown]
contribution = 1–50 {actual number of years contribution}
contribution_period = [< = 10; 10–22; 23–25; 25+]
error1 = "contribution period must be greater than zero"
error2 = "no age given"
error3 = "no age and no preferred retirement age given"
age = 18–65
preferred_retirement_age = 40–65
sex = [male; female]

Figure 9.11   Object dictionary built from the DFDs and decision trees.

9.9 CONCLUSION

In this chapter, consideration has been given to how a number of techniques from traditional systems analysis and design might be adapted to the exigencies of knowledge engineering – the building of knowledge base systems.

E–R diagramming is primarily a technique for representing declarative knowledge – the set of objects, attributes and values present in a given knowledge domain. Object dictionaries are a non-graphic technique for representing more detailed information about factual frameworks.

Data-flow diagramming is a useful technique for representing procedural knowledge. In particular, it is a useful technique to employ in partitioning a system into modular knowledge bases. Decision trees are a complementary technique which are useful for graphically representing the structure of rule sets.

All these techniques should be an essential part of any knowledge engineer's toolkit for three major reasons:

1. All such techniques act as a useful means for documenting knowledge and discussing such knowledge more easily with domain experts than traditional rule sets.
2. All such techniques encourage knowledge engineers to engage in some detailed conceptual modelling prior to implementing a first prototype.
3. They encourage the knowledge engineer to consider useful interactions between KBS and more conventional systems.

9.10 RECALL EXERCISES

1. What are the benefits of adapting conventional systems analysis techniques to knowledge engineering?
2. What is an entity–relationship diagram?

3. What is a data-flow diagram and in what way is it applicable to knowledge engineering?
4. What is a decision tree?
5. What is an object dictionary?
6. What is meant by the distinction between declarative and procedural knowledge?

9.11 OPEN-ENDED QUESTIONS

1. Data-flow diagrams are primarily a technique for partitioning large knowledge base systems. Discuss.
2. Discuss how adapting techniques from conventional information systems work encourages the production of embedded knowledge base systems.
3. In what way are E–R diagrams a distinct technique from NIAM and conceptual graphs?

REFERENCES

Addis T.R. (1987). *Designing Knowledge Base Systems*. Kogan Page, London.

Beynon-Davies P. (1989). *Information Systems Development*. Macmillan, London.

Beynon-Davies P. (to be published 1992). *Relational Database Design*. Blackwell Scientific, Oxford.

Chen P.P-S. (1976). The entity–relationship model – Toward a unified view of data. *ACM Trans. on Database Systems*, **1**(1), 9–36.

Cutts G. (1991). *Structured Systems Analysis and Design Methodology*, 2nd Edn. Blackwell Scientific, Oxford.

De-Marco T. (1979). *Structured Analysis and System Specification*. Prentice-Hall, Englewood Cliffs, NJ.

Finkelstein C. (1989). *An Introduction to Information Engineering: from Strategic Planning to Information Systems*. Addison-Wesley, Sydney.

Gane C. and Sarson T. (1977). *Structured Systems Analysis: Tools and Techniques*. Prentice-Hall, Englewood Cliffs, NJ.

Howe D.R. (1983). *Data Analysis for Data Base Design*. Edward Arnold, London.

Keller R. (1987). *Expert System Technology – Development and Application*. Yourdon Press, NY.

Swaffield G. and Knight B. (1990). Applying systems analysis techniques to knowledge engineering. *Expert Systems*, **7**(2), 82–93.

OBJECT ANALYSIS: AN INTEGRATED APPROACH TO KNOWLEDGE ANALYSIS AND DOCUMENTATION

10.1 INTRODUCTION

Object-oriented (OO) is definitely the current thing to be. Systems analysis, systems design, programming and, most recently, database systems have all been caught up in the crest of this new wave. Roger King (King, 1988) has even written an article entitled *My Cat is Object-Oriented*. The implication being that if his cat is OO then he is far more likely to be able to sell it!

This chapter is an attempt to apply some much-needed cautious consideration to the contemporary hype surrounding OO. In particular, it will demonstrate how much of the OO paradigm can be seen as a natural extension of, or evolution from, techniques that have been applied in the information systems world for a number of years.

The main aim of the chapter is to portray how conceptual modelling as applied to database systems can move relatively painlessly into the domain of OO. It will discuss how OO analysis, an approach primarily directed at the building of applications in procedural or object-oriented languages, is equally relevant to the development of database systems, expert systems and expert database systems. The intention is to site the techniques firmly in the history of semantic data modelling.

10.2 SEMANTIC DATA MODELS

In Chapter 3 we described a semantic data model (SDM) as being an attempt to provide a more expressive means of representing the meaning of information than is available in classic data models such as the relational data model. In this sense, SDMs come closer to providing a mechanism for the storage of information – data plus semantics.

SDMs have contributed in two senses to the development of OO. First, as a means of specifying the architecture of advanced database management systems (DBMS) (Brown, 1991). Second, as a discipline for the analysis and design of database systems. In the first sense, SDMs have spawned many of the developments in the current crop of OO DBMS. In the second sense, SDMs have spawned at least one branch of the current crop of OO analysis methodologies.

10.3 STREAMS OF OO ANALYSIS

Most paradigms are based on a small number of firmly held principles. One of the principles which is adopted in most of the contemporary literature on OO is that: *the objective of OO development is to heal the contemporary divide between process analysis methods and data analysis methods.*

Proponents of OO rightly point to the deficiencies of each of the contemporary approaches to information systems development (Yourdon, 1990). Process analysis methods based around techniques such as data-flow diagramming over-emphasize the functional or dynamic side of information systems and under-emphasize the structural or static side of information systems. In contrast, data analysis methods based on such techniques as entity–relationship diagramming over-emphasize data and under-emphasize process.

Since objects, as we shall see, have both a structural (data) and behavioural (process) aspect, any analysis method based on such concepts should reflect the integrative emphasis of objects. However, it is interesting to note that few of the proposed OO methods divorce themselves entirely from the 'structured' battles of the 1980s. Most of the current OO methods pay lip-service to having some ancestry in the process-oriented or data-oriented traditions. What we might call process-directed OO methods build objects out of clusters of behaviours or functions (Gibson, 1990). In contrast, data-driven OO methods start with an analysis of structure and introduce functions later (Coad and Yourdon, 1991).

Since our objective in this chapter is to outline OO contributions to database and knowledge base development we shall move with the data-driven stream. Our aim is:

1. To demonstrate how a relatively seamless join is feasible between classic database design technologies and emerging OO methods. To do this we review the idea of an entity model discussed in the previous chapter.
2. To demonstrate how the extension of an entity model into an object model offers promise of an integrative approach to the problems of knowledge base development.

10.4 ENTITY MODELS

An entity model is a model of the entities and relationships in some domain of discourse. An entity may be defined as 'a thing which the enterprise recognizes as being capable of an independent existence and which can be uniquely identified'. A relationship can be defined as 'an association between two or more entities' (Beynon-Davies, 1992).

Although the term entity is the one most commonly used, following Chen (1976) we should really speak of an entity type. An entity type is a category. There is only one instance of an entity type. An entity, strictly speaking, is an instance of a given entity type. There are usually many instances of entities.

Entity models are usually mapped out as entity–relationship diagrams. The end-product of entity–relationship diagramming is a model of the entities and relationships in a particular application environment (see Chapter 9).

10.5 ENTITIES TO OBJECTS

Entity modelling as we have described it in this, and the previous chapter, has much in common with object modelling (Blaha *et al.*, 1988). In this section we consider some of the common threads between entity and object modelling and discuss some proposals for extending entity modelling into an object modelling approach.

Above, we defined an entity as being some thing of interest to an organization which has an independent existence. This abstract definition can serve equally well for defining objects. The major difference between entities and objects lies in the way we apply these constructs in the modelling process. Entities are primarily static constructs. An entity model gives us a useful framework for painting the structural detail of a database system. In other words, an entity model translates into declarative knowledge: a framework for facts.

Objects, however, have a more ambitious purpose. An object is designed to encapsulate both a structural and a behavioural aspect. In other words, an object model gives us a means for designing not only a database structure but also how that database structure is to be used. An object model not only models facts, it also models rules, and can be used to model processes of inference.

The easiest way to begin to build an object model is to exploit some of the inherent strengths of entity modelling and extend them with some behavioural abstractions.

10.6 OBJECT MODELS

In this section we shall discuss an approach to OO analysis which builds directly on some of the extensions to entity modelling discussed in Chapter 9.

An object model is built from the following components: objects, methods and messages. An object is a package of data and procedures. Data are contained in attributes of an object. Procedures are defined by an object's methods. Methods are activated by messages passed between objects.

In the same way as we distinguish between entities and entity types, we should strictly distinguish between an object and an object class. An object class is a grouping of similar objects that define their attributes and methods. Objects are instances of some class. They have the same attributes and methods. In other words, object classes define the intension of the database – the central topic of database design. Objects define the extension of a database – the central topic of database implementation.

The primary reason for defining objects in this manner is that they should display a property known as encapsulation, sometimes known as information hiding. This is the process of packaging together both data and process with a defined boundary and controlled access across that boundary.

Every object should be distinguishable from every other object. This is achieved by assigning each object a unique identity. We follow the practice of assigning an object identifier to each object class.

10.7 OBJECTS AT CYMRO

To change the context of our case study slightly, let us begin to apply OO analysis to another aspect of the business of the Cymro building society. Let us suppose that Cymro maintain a number of distinct types of building society account: OrdinaryShare, Instant-Xtra, 90DaysXtra, MonthlyIncome, GoldAccount and Tessa. Each type of account is designed to suit the profile of a particular type of customer.

Cymro management have decided that they wish to build an integrated expert database system to help administer and extend this side of their business. The database system will record details of existing customers and their investments, and it is proposed that this database will reside on the company's central mainframe. An expert system is planned that will enable staff at the branches to advise the right type of account for the right customer. The accounts advisor, as it is to be known, will reside on a PC platform but will have links to the mainframe. Information on new accounts will be downloaded to the investment database from the accounts advisor.

Knowledge analysis consists of conducting a number of interviews with suitable domain experts. We summarize the information gained in the following transcript:

> We offer six different types of account at our building society: OrdinaryShare, InstantXtra, 90DaysExtra, MonthlyIncome, GoldAccount and our Tessa. These accounts are distinguished in terms of the minimum investment required, the amount of access needed to the money, whether a regular income is required from the interest paid to the account, and whether tax exemption is required.
>
> The Ordinary Share, InstantXtra and 90DaysExtra account pay no income. All interest earned on monies in such accounts is reinvested in the accounts. Both OrdinaryShare and InstantXtra allow instant access to the money in such accounts. The 90DaysExtra demands that you give three months notice of withdrawal. You need just £50 to open an Ordinary-Share, and £500 to open an InstantXtra or 90DaysXtra. Interest on OrdinaryShare accounts is currently 7% gross; InstantXtra 8.5% gross and 90DaysXtra 9.5% gross.
>
> Two other accounts are designed for income generation every month. To open a MonthlyIncome account you need a minimum of £10 000 to invest. It pays interest at 10.5% gross. To open a GoldAccount you need a minimum of £25 000 to invest. It pays interest at 12% gross.
>
> The last account offered is a Tessa. This is a tax-exempt savings scheme. Customers have to invest a minimum of £500 for a period of five years. Interest is paid at 11%.

Figure 10.1 summarizes this knowledge as a generalization hierarchy in the notation of an extended E–R diagram. Note how all building society accounts (the class BuildAccount) have attributes such as InterestRate and MinimumInvestment in common. Only access accounts, however, are designed for easy withdrawal, and only income accounts are designed for regular payments to customers. This distinction is drawn through the class AccessAccount maintaining an Access attribute and the class IncomeAccount maintaining an Income attribute.

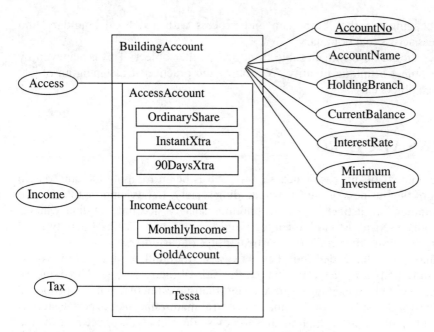

Figure 10.1 Extended E–R diagram representing obtained knowledge as a generalization hierarchy.

Fig. 10.2 shows how the structural detail is drawn for OrdinaryShare and Monthly-Income accounts. Note how we distinguish between distributive and collective properties of a class. In Fig. 10.2, AccountNo, AccountName, HoldingBranch, and CurrentBalance are all distributive attributes of the class OrdinaryShare. Each OrdinaryShare account will inherit these attributes, but each object will fill these attributes differently. InterestRate, MinimumInvestment and Access are, however, collective attributes of the class. The values assigned to these attributes are true for all members of the class.

10.8 BEHAVIOURAL MECHANISMS

As well as structural detail, each object has a defined interface which specifies its behaviour. We indicate such an interface by drawing a rounded box around the appropriate entity symbol. All communication with an object takes place via this interface.

Two major types of behavioural mechanism need to be documented in the design of a database system: constraints and transactions. Constraints define allowable states of a database. Transactions are the means of causing changes to a database. Constraints and transactions are therefore interdependent. Constraints determine the acceptable behaviour of transactions. Transactions are the means of activating constraints.

This interdependence is reflected in an object model. Transactions are represented

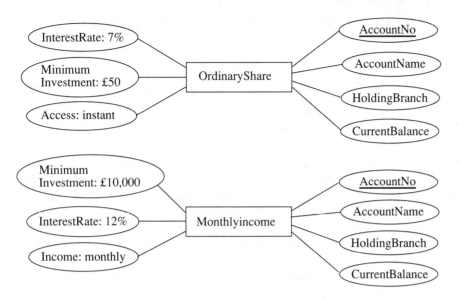

Figure 10.2 Representation of structural detail for OrdinaryShare and MonthlyIncome accounts.

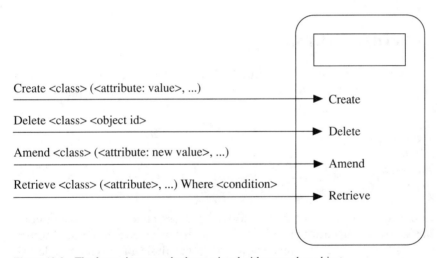

Figure 10.3 The four primary methods associated with every class object.

usually by messages between objects. Constraints are generally embedded in the methods pertaining to objects. Messages activate the methods associated with an object.

Every class object has associated with it four primary methods: Create, Delete, Amend and Retrieve (see Fig. 10.3). These correspond to the classic file maintenance operations or transaction types implemented in most DBMS. Because of their ubiquity such methods are usually left off the diagrams pertaining to object models. However, if constraints are attached to such methods then the primary method concerned should be displayed on the object diagram.

For instance, we might attach an existence constraint to the Create method of the class BuildAccount to the effect that:

a BuildAccount should not be created for a non-existent Customer

We might also attach a similar type of constraint to the delete method of the Customer class to the effect that:

a Customer object should not be deleted until all associated BuildAccount objects have been deleted.

An object class may have several secondary methods defined within it. Secondary methods are always written on the object diagram. We have defined three methods for the object class in Fig. 10.4: Credit, Debit and ChangeRate. Methods provide the link between data and transactions. In a truly OO manner, transactions impact upon data (attributes) through messages. Credits and Debits, for instance, are messages which activate the methods of the object class and update the CurrentBalance attributes of object instances.

Secondary methods may also be used to incorporate integrity constraints. Hence the Debit method might incorporate a check on an account's current balance. Fig. 10.4 illustrates a message dependency (indicated by the arrow) between a Customer class and a BankAccount class.

10.9 STAGES IN OO ANALYSIS

OO analysis is strongly iterative in nature. Although the technique can be described in terms of the following stages, the process is one of successive refinement with numerous feedback loops.

1. Identify object classes.
2. Identify attributes.
3. Identify relationships.
4. Identify messages/methods.

In most traditional approaches to database design, process concerns are introduced either as a means of validating entity models, or as a means of recording physical design decisions against entity models. The main benefit that OO analysis offers database design is the ability to integrate at the logical level behavioural with structural concerns.

10.10 ACCOMMODATION TO THE RELATIONAL MODEL

In much the same way that entity models are naturally implementable in entity–relationship databases, object models are most naturally implementable in OO databases. However, the level of abstraction built into object models means that, like entity models, object models can be accommodated to relational schema. Some of the steps involved are indicated below:

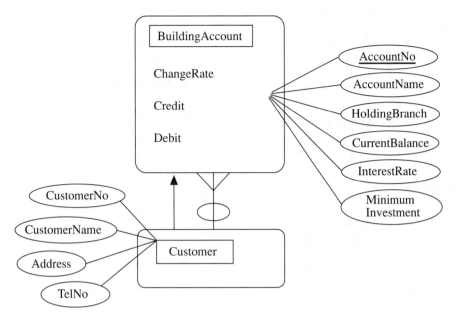

Figure 10.4 Secondary methods defined within the object class.

1. Each object becomes a relation.
2. The object ID becomes the primary key of the relation.
3. All other attributes become non-key data-items of the table.
4. Each 1:M association between objects is implemented via a foreign key (object ID) at the many end of a relationship.
5. Optional status at the many end of an association means that the foreign key should be declared null.
6. Superclasses and subclasses form separate relations with the same object ID.
7. Inheritance can be simulated via views (Kung, 1990).
8. In the near future methods will be implementable in the extended integrity language of SQL. For the moment, constraints need to be implemented in code written in some host language such as C or some applications building tool such as ORACLE's SQL*FORMS.
9. Messages translate into major transactions. Primary or secondary methods without constraints can be implemented in the basic file maintenance primitives of SQL. Complex transactions involving the activation of numerous constraints will need to be produced in a host language.

A schema for the customers and investments database will be constructed in Chapter 11.

10.11 THE ACCOUNTS ADVISOR

Having developed an object model for the customers and investments database, we now need to develop a model for the building society accounts advisor. To emphasize the

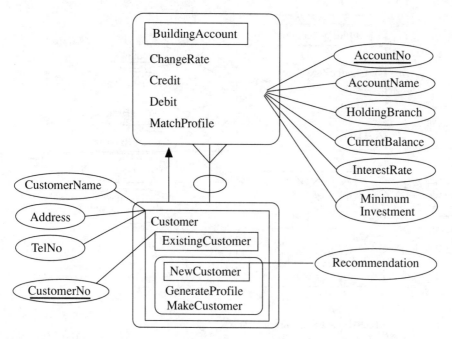

Figure 10.5   Development of an object model for the building society accounts advisor.

integration of expert and database system we conduct this analysis via incremental adjustments to our existing object model.

Let us begin by distinguishing between two types of customer: existing customers and new customers. Existing customers have already been represented in the object model. Existing customers are persons who already hold accounts with Cymro. In contrast, new customers are those persons who do not hold any investments with the building society. Consequently, new customers have not been assigned any CustomerNo. This distinction is illustrated in Fig. 10.5.

We have added three new methods to this model: MatchProfile in the class BuildAccount; GenerateProfile and MakeCustomer in the NewCustomer class. We have also added a recommendation attribute to the class NewCustomer. All such amendments are meant to facilitate the construction of the Accounts Advisor:

1. GenerateProfile is a method which collects relevant details about a new customer: the amount he or she has to invest; the degree of access required to the invested money; whether a regular income is required to the money; whether tax exemption is important. After details are collected, a message is sent to the class BuildAccount activating the MatchProfile method.
2. The MatchProfile method performs an iteration on the members of the set of building society accounts. If a match is found it returns a value or set of values. The GenerateProfile method then updates the recommendation attribute.
3. If the customer decides he or she wishes to invest, then the MakeCustomer method is activated. This transforms a new customer into an existing customer by generating a CustomerNo and taking such details as name, address, telephone number, etc.

10.12 CONCLUSION

We summarize the discussion below:

1. Entity models, as represented by entity–relationship diagrams, can evolve into object models, as represented by object diagrams.
2. Object models are equivalent to entity models plus two additional sets of abstraction mechanisms:
   (a) structural abstraction such as generalization and aggregation;
   (b) behavioural abstraction such as methods and messages.
3. Object models provide a new dimension for database design. They allow the integration of process analysis with the proven traditions of structural analysis.
4. Object models can be used to develop the newer OO databases or more conventional databases, such as relational systems. An accommodation process for relational schema has been provided.
5. Object models are equally relevant for specifying the components of expert systems, and are particularly well-suited to emphasizing the integration of expert and database systems.

10.13 RECALL EXERCISES

1. What are the two major streams of OO analysis?
2. Distinguish between an entity and an object.
3. Distinguish between an entity model and an object model.
4. What is meant by encapsulation?
5. Distinguish between a method and a message.
6. Describe the main steps in producing a relational scheme from an object diagram.
7. How might we incorporate the following amendment into the building society account model: *an existing customer may also be a new customer; he may be looking for a new investment?*

10.14 OPEN-ENDED EXERCISES

1. In what way can object analysis be regarded as an integrated approach to knowledge analysis and documentation?
2. Discuss the similarities with and differences between object analysis and:
   (a) dependency diagramming;
   (b) NIAM;
   (c) conceptual graphs.
3. What techniques are appropriate for managing the complexity associated with large object models?
4. In the 1970s and early 1980s, structured development was on the rising edge of a hype curve. Today, structured development is treated with more pragmatism. We have learned some of the strengths and weaknesses of structured techniques. Will OO analysis follow a similar progression on a hype curve?

REFERENCES

Beynon-Davies P. (1992). *Relational Database Design*. Blackwell Scientific, Oxford.

Blaha M.R., Premerlani W.J. and Rumbaugh J.E. (1988). Relational database design using an object-oriented methodology Comm. ACM, **31**(4), 414–427.

Brown A. (1991). *Object-Oriented Databases: Applications in Software Engineering*. McGraw-Hill, London.

Chen P.P-S. (1976). The entity–relationship model – toward a unified view of data. *ACM Trans. on Database Systems*, **1**(1), 9–36.

Coad P. and Yourdon E. (1991). *Object-Oriented Analysis*. 2nd Edn. Prentice-Hall, Englewood-Cliffs, NJ.

Gibson E. (1990). Born and bred: object behaviour analysis. *Byte*, Oct, 245–254.

King R. (1988). My cat is object-oriented. In Kim W. and Lochovsky F. *Object-Oriented Languages, Applications and Databases*. Addison-Wesley, Reading, MA.

Kung C. (1990). Object subclass hierarchy in SQL: a simple approach. *Comm. ACM*, **33**(7), 117–125.

Yourdon E. (1990). Auld Lang Syne. *Byte*, Oct, 257–261.

11

DEVELOPING KNOWLEDGE BASE SYSTEMS

11.1 INTRODUCTION

A major theme of this book has been that the differences between knowledge engineering, software engineering and information engineering have been over-emphasized. We return to this issue once again. This chapter discusses how the developers of expert systems, particularly the users of expert system shells as discussed in Chapter 4, would be better served by an emphasis on the similarities between the two disciplines.

Shells, much like fourth-generation languages, often invite you to run before you can walk. They invite you to take a 'suck it and see' approach to systems development. We have discussed in a previous chapter some of the problems inherent in this approach. We also discussed how traditional software developers have long emphasized the importance of prior considered analysis and design before enthusiastic coding. The same is true for the development of expert systems.

In this chapter we consider the remaining stages of the knowledge base system development life-cycle: design, implementation, evaluation and maintenance.

11.2 DFDS TO KNOWLEDGE BASES

In Chapter 9 we discussed how data-flow diagrams (DFDs) can be used to document the procedural aspects of knowledge in a particular domain. One conclusion we came to was that each process box on a diagram can be regarded as a rule set. In this section we consider a number of heuristics for determining the required make-up of any given rule set.

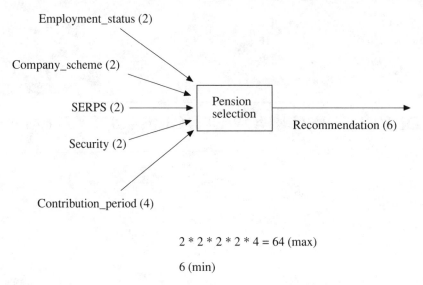

$$2 * 2 * 2 * 2 * 4 = 64 \text{ (max)}$$

$$6 \text{ (min)}$$

Figure 11.1   Calculating the number of rules for the pension selection process.

Consider the pension selection process in Fig. 11.1. Five objects input to the process and one object outputs. Each of the input objects has a number of allowed values. This tells us that the maximum number of rules we should need for this rule set would be the multiplication of these values. Alternatively, our output object has six possible values it can take. This tells us that we would need a minimum of six rules to fully cover this rule set, if only one conclusion is allowed per rule.

Most practicable rule sets lie between these maxima and minima. If the number of input attributes were to increase by only a small number then the maxima would increase astronomically. Fortunately, some of the combinations of input values will not apply. Most designs for rule bases therefore use the logical connectives *and* and *or* to reduce the size of the rule set.

11.3 DECISION TREES TO RULE SETS

In Chapter 9 we outlined how a process box on our DFD can be represented by a decision tree. A decision tree is merely a graphical representation of a rule set. We can translate a decision tree into a rule set by using a simple algorithm. Each branch of our decision tree from the top-most node to a leaf node constitutes a rule. Hence the following rule set constitutes the branches of the decision tree represented in Fig. 9.9.

IF employmentStatus is selfEmployed
AND contributionPeriod > 10
THEN recommendation is amicable

IF employmentStatus is selfEmployed
AND contributionPeriod $\leqslant$ 10
THEN recommendation is premiumAccount

IF employmentStatus is employed
AND companyScheme is yes
AND serps is yes
THEN recommendation is premiumAccount

IF employmentStatus is employed
AND companyScheme is yes
AND serps is no
THEN recommendation is stayInScheme

IF employmentStatus is employed
AND companyScheme is no
AND serps is no
THEN recommendation is checkDetails

IF employmentStatus is employed
AND companyScheme is no
AND serps is yes
AND contributionPeriod $\geqslant$ 25
THEN recommendation is equitable

IF employmentStatus is employed
AND companyScheme is no
AND serps is yes
AND contributionPeriod $<$ 25
AND contributionPeriod $\geqslant$ 22
AND security is high
THEN recommendation is equitable

IF employmentStatus is employed
AND companyScheme is no
AND serps is yes
AND contributionPeriod $<$ 25
AND contributionPeriod $\geqslant$ 22
AND security is low
THEN recommendation is prudent

IF employmentStatus is employed
AND companyScheme is no
AND serps is yes
AND contributionPeriod $<$ 25
AND contributionPeriod $\geqslant$ 22
AND security is unknown
THEN recommendation is prudent

IF employmentStatus is employed
AND companyScheme is no
AND serps is yes
AND contributionPeriod < 25
AND contributionPeriod ≥ 10
THEN recommendation is prudent

IF employmentStatus is employed
AND companyScheme is no
AND serps is yes
AND contributionPeriod < 10
THEN recommendation is premiumAccount

11.4 OBJECT DICTIONARIES TO FRAMES

The object dictionaries described in Chapter 9 bear a close resemblance to structured objects as discussed in Chapter 3. This means that each definition in our object dictionary can be turned into a frame for an object. Hence, we might construct a frame for *employmentStatus*, *contributionPeriod* and *recommendation* as follows:

Name: employmentStatus
Type: text
Description: employed by a company or own employment
Values: employed, selfEmployed
Default: employed

Name: contributionPeriod
Type: numeric
Description: number of probable years contribution
Values: < 10, 10–22, 23–25, > 25
Default: 10–22

Name: recommendation
Type: text
Description: recommended personal pension
Values: prudent, amicable, equitable, premiumAccount, stayInScheme, checkDetails
Default: equitable

11.5 OBJECT DIAGRAMS TO EXPERT DATABASE SYSTEMS

In this section we discuss how the object model produced in Chapter 10 can be used to produce a design for an integrated database and expert system. The object model, at least as far as the database is concerned, would achieve its most natural implementation in an OODBMS. However, in this section we discuss a relational implementation of object modelling concepts.

First, the object diagram in Fig. 10.1 can be used to design a relational database for customers and accounts information according to the steps described in Section 10.10. The relational schema is given below:

Customers(*customerNo*, customerName, address)
BuildingAccounts(*accountNo*, accountName, customerNo, holdingBranch, currentBalance, interestRate, minimumInvestment)
AccessAccounts(*accountNo*, access)
IncomeAccounts(*accountNo*, income)
Tessas(*accountNo*, tax)

Also, we can simulate inheritance between the class BuildingAccount, the class AccessAccount and OrdinaryShare accounts by using the following view:

CREATE VIEW OrdinaryShare AS
SELECT B.accountNo, holdingBranch, interestRate, currentBalance
FROM BuildAccounts B, AccessAccounts A
WHERE B.accountNo = A.accountNo AND accountName = 'OrdinaryShare'

We can simulate the method Credit with the following SQL script:

/*CREDIT.SQL*/
UPDATE BuildAccounts
SET currentBalance = currentBalance + &1
WHERE accountNo = &2

The methods MatchProfile and GenerateProfile that form the heart of the Accounts Advisor could be implemented in a number of different ways. We defer this discussion until Section 11.7.

11.6 DESIGN AND AUTOMATIC KNOWLEDGE ACQUISITION

The notion of designing a knowledge base through the application of appropriate partitioning seems at first glance to be very similar to the exercise performed by such rule-induction algorithms as ID3 (see Section 7.5). This is not surprising when one realizes that, to use ID3 effectively, one still needs to first define the objects and values relevant to the objects in the particular domain. Bloomfield has argued, however, that the problem of providing relevant objects is unsuitable for consideration by domain experts alone (Bloomfield, 1986). A better method is to feed off the fruitful interactions between a domain expert skilled in the field under study, and a knowledge engineer skilled in building knowledge base systems.

Once such objects and values are defined, they are related with the overall goal of the system through an analysis of their discriminatory power. To do this, a training set of examples must be supplied to the rule-induction system which uses this material to partition the attributes of the domain. Such partitioning, however, is purely a reflection of the status of the training set. If the training set is ill-considered or incomplete, the rules generated by the system will be ill-considered or incomplete.

This leads one to the conclusion that although rule induction is a useful aid in the development of expert systems, it does not replace the important role for the knowledge engineer in designing knowledge base systems in the manner described in this chapter.

11.7 IMPLEMENTING KNOWLEDGE BASE SYSTEMS

In Chapters 3 and 4 we discussed a number of distinct ways of representing knowledge. In this section we discuss how these might be applied to the pension system.

The rules in Section 11.3 illustrate how the pension system might be implemented as a series of production rules, probably in the syntax of some expert system shell. Such rules would be supplemented with a series of frames describing such properties of objects as allowed values and defaults as described in Section 11.4. This implementation would probably run in standalone mode. In other words, the user would be continuously prompted for customer details.

A contrasting approach would be to design a database for customer information based on the dependency analysis discussed in Section 8.4 (Arbanel and Williams, 1987). The tables in Fig. 11.2 illustrate a simplification of this database.

The Customers table displays a subset of customer information used to make recommendations. The Rules table implements the *if* and *then* parts of production rules as record structures. A simple join between these two tables using a SQL statement such as the one below would be sufficient to emulate a forward-chaining inference mechanism.

(a) Customers

customer number	contribution period	employment status	company scheme	serps	security
01	15	selfEmployed			
02	20	employed	yes		
03	23	selfEmployed	no	yes	high
04	30	selfEmployed	yes	yes	

(b) Rules

rule no	employment status	contribution low	high	company scheme	serps	security	recommendation
01	selfEmployed	11	50				amicable
02	selfEmployed	0	10				premiumAccount
03	employed	0	50	yes	yes		premiumAccount
04	employed	0	50	yes	no		stayInScheme
05	employed	0	50	no	no		checkDetails
06	employed	25	50	no	yes		equitable
07	employed	22	25	no	yes	high	equitable
08	employed	22	25	no	yes	low	prudent
09	employed	22	25	no	yes		prudent
10	employed	0	9	no	yes		premiumAccount

Figure 11.2 Simplified database for customer information.

```
select customerNo, ruleNo, recommendation
from customers, rules
where customers.companyScheme  =  rules.companyScheme
and customers.serps  =  rules.serps
and customers.security  =  rules.security
and customers.contributionPeriod between contributionLow and contributionHigh
```

Yet another approach would be offered by a Postgres-like active database facility. Using much the same database, a series of update statements could be declared as described in Chapter 4. This approach, which is illustrated below, could be similarly implemented using a language such as C with appropriate external file access.

```
Customers(customerNo, sname, fname, address, maritalStatus, homePhone,
workPhone, DOB, occupation, salary, sex, serps, preferredRetirement,
companyScheme, security, recommendation)
Occupations(occupation, employmentStatus)

CREATE VIEW customer–view
AS SELECT preferredRetirement–(sysdate–DOB) contributionPeriod
serps, companyScheme, security, employmentStatus, recommendation
FROM customers C, occupations O
WHERE c.ooccupation = O.occupation

ALWAYS UPDATE customer–view
SET recommendation = 'amicable'
WHERE employmentStatus = 'self–employed'
AND contributionPeriod ⩾ 10

ALWAYS UPDATE customer–view
SET recommendation = 'premium–account'
WHERE employmentStatus = 'self–employed'
AND contributionPeriod < 10
```

The advantage of both database approaches is their persistent quality. The data held in the database could be used for other corporate purposes such as customer analyses or mailing lists.

11.8 EVALUATING KNOWLEDGE BASE SYSTEMS

The evaluation of knowledge base systems is a term which covers methods for system verification, validation and usability (Preece, 1990).

1. Verification. The term verification in conventional software engineering is the method of determining whether an implemented system satisfies its specification. In much knowledge engineering work it has not proven possible to fully specify an expert

system before implementation. Verification is therefore normally carried out to ensure that an expert system is internally self-consistent and complete.

2. Validation. Validation of systems is carried out to determine whether or not a system performs the tasks for which it was created. Validation looks at the utility of the system. It refers to the quality of a system's advice and decisions.

3. Usability. Usability or user acceptance testing generally refers to the ergonomic and organizational aspects of a system. It refers not only to the quality of human–computer interaction but also to ideas of a system's efficiency and cost-effectiveness.

Most papers reporting the results of expert system projects have described methods for verification and/or validation. Berry and Hart (1990) is a useful overview of work done on the usability of expert systems.

The most popular method of verification involves running a set of test cases on an expert system and assessing the accuracy of the results. This will be discussed in the next section.

However, the ultimate criterion of success for most expert systems is whether they will be used effectively. A key ingredient in ensuring such success has been shown to be the involvement of users in the evaluation of a system as it is being built. Such evaluations can help to determine the utility of a system, the extent of its capabilities, its ease of interaction, the intelligibility and credibility of its results, its efficiency, speed and reliability.

Consequently, Suen *et al.* (1990) have argued that evaluation is not something that occurs at the end of an expert system project. They stress the need for system evluation throughout the entire development process.

11.9 MAINTAINING KNOWLEDGE BASE SYSTEMS

It is important to realize that most useful knowledge base systems, like useful software systems in general, will probably never reach a state of completion. The problem of maintenance is therefore of equal significance to knowledge bases as it has been to conventional databases.

The traditional issues of testing, debugging and modifying a knowledge base will be presented here as separate topics. In real life, they are of course interwoven under the all-encompassing concept of maintenance.

11.9.1 Testing a knowledge base

Most of the expert systems built to date have not been rigorously tested. For those that have undergone some form of evaluation, the usual approach has been to compare a human expert with the expert system on a selection of tasks from the problem domain.

Using this approach, testing a knowledge base system involves first eliciting a suitable collection of task material from the experts in the domain – what we might call a test-bed. Each case or example within such a test-bed has two aspects:

1. It details the information to be input to the expert system.
2. It specifies the requisite output given the particular conditions that prevail. This

normally means specifying the conclusion or conclusions that the expert system should come to. For example, in terms of our pension expert system, a suitable test-bed would be made up of a number of customer profiles together with the recommendation arrived at in each case.

The test-bed is normally expected to consist of material which varies in complexity. Simple material is run on the system first, more complex material is run on the system later.

11.9.2 Debugging problems

Testing a knowledge base in this manner will probably reveal a number of problems. For instance:

1. There may be gaps in the knowledge.
2. Rules may overlap, leading to inconsistent and redundant conclusions.
3. Rules probably interact in unsuspected but deleterious ways.

The traditional test model for knowledge base systems has been to treat the entire expert system as a black box. Facts are fed in at one end, and conclusions are checked at the other end. The problem with this approach is that it is usually extremely difficult to work back from a particular erroneous conclusion to the mechanisms that produced it.

A number of machine aids have been developed to ease this task. For instance, a reasoning trace which details the path the system has taken through the knowledge base can be extremely useful. Tools are also available to check on such things as the logical consistency of the rules in a knowledge base. Even with such tools, however, debugging a large knowledge base is no easy task.

Such problems are really symptoms of the monolithic approach described above. In this book we have continually emphasized the importance of partitioning the knowledge base. Partitioning has benefits which feed into the analysis, design and programming of systems. It also has other important benefits in the area of testing.

For example, rather than testing a large knowledge base as a single entity, a partitioned knowledge base can be tested 'incrementally'. By this we mean that for each of the modules that make up our knowledge base, we generate a suitable mini test-bed of examples. We then use this material to test each module independently. When we are happy that each module performs its function satisfactorily, we then start to build up the system a module at a time. The emphasis therefore changes from considering the internal 'cohesion' of modules to the external 'coupling' between modules (Yourdon, 1977). In doing this, therefore, we need material that will thoroughly test module interactions.

Such an incremental approach to testing makes the process far more manageable. This is because, the 'depth of inference' in a module will be several times smaller than in the full system. This makes such modules far easier to understand and maintain.

11.9.3 Amending the knowledge base

Alongside the problems of debugging a knowledge base (i.e. locating the source of system malfunctions) there lie the associated problems of amending, modifying or correcting the knowledge base. For instance:

1. Whenever a change is made to part of an expert system, the change must be propagated through all parts of that system. The knowledge engineer must therefore take great care to ensure that he can find all the associated amendments that need to be made.
2. As the size of the knowledge base grows, the knowledge engineer will probably lose his understanding of the system as a whole.
3. Rules are often not strictly independent. There may be subtle and hidden assumptions concealed in the order they are listed in the knowledge base. A change in the order of the rule base may therefore have effects that may not have been foreseen.

Partitioning or modularizing the knowledge base in the manner described in the previous chapter can ease some of the problems described above. For instance, one of the major emphases of data-flow diagramming is the attempt to define relatively independent modules that can be maintained as individual units. This means that if we need to make amendments to the knowledge base, it should be relatively straightforward for us to decide to which module or modules such amendments need to be made, and more importantly, it should also be equally clear what effect such amendments will have on the changed modules. In other words, partitioning is fundamentally about effectively managing inter-module interactions.

Having said this, partitioning is not the be-all and end-all of effective maintenance. There are a number of other things that can be done about the problems described which have more to do with project-team control. For instance, it must be said that few knowledge base systems have yet been in continual use in real environments for substantial periods of time. When knowledge base systems achieve more acceptance, particularly in the commercial world, there will be new difficulties associated with successive generations of personnel coping with a continually evolving system. New knowledge engineers may, for example, need to alter a system that has been built by a previous team. The structure of the system must be very explicit if they are to be able to do this easily.

In previous chapters we emphasized the importance of documenting knowledge in a form other than the elements of a knowledge base. The importance of this exercise is nowhere better felt than in the area of maintenance. In the expert systems literature, people are encouraged to keep records of the reasons for writing or changing any rules. They are also asked to keep records of the author and date of a new rule or rule change. This is really an instance of good project management. The author believes, however, that much more than this needs to be undertaken whenever a change is made to the knowledge base. Team-members must continually update the specification of the system, perhaps in terms of system DFDs, E–R diagrams, object dictionaries or object diagrams. In other words, the specification of the system must continually reflect the status of the knowledge base.

Using manual methods, this is clearly an onerous task. Adapting some of the automated methods available in conventional information systems work may, however, make this a much more practical undertaking.

11.10 KNOWLEDGE BASE SYSTEMS AND ORGANIZATIONS

The most discussed person in the expert systems literature is the domain expert. Evaluation, for instance, is cast usually as ensuring that the domain expert agrees with the conclusions of a given expert system. However, the point is frequently missed that many domain experts will never actually use an implemented system. Most commercial expert systems are designed for use by non-experts. It is to this much-neglected topic of the user and user involvement that we now turn.

In commerce and industry, an expert system will be introduced into a work situation made up of people with existing attitudes to technology, an industrial relations climate that may be positive or negative, and a set of long-established management–worker and worker–worker relationships. All these factors will affect the way in which the expert system is received and used. Its technical merit may have little to do with its acceptability and use. Also, whereas previous computing developments have had their impact on the lower levels of the labour force such as clerks, expert systems affect many of the professional groups such as doctors, dentists and lawyers. Professional groups have usually achieved excellent results in the past in protecting their own interests.

Human problems such as the above must be tackled at the core of an expert systems project. One way towards achieving this is to build a high degree of user involvement into a project. Mumford (1985), for instance, describes a project conducted by the Intelligent Systems Technologies Group of Digital Equipment. This project used a design methodology developed by Mumford known as ETHICS (Effective Technical and Human Implementation of Computer-Based Systems) which is an approach that emphasizes the importance of job satisfaction and work design. The approach at Digital proceeded as follows:

1. A project group was created consisting of experts, knowledge engineers and users.
2. The group was trained in technical and organizational skills as well as the philosophy of participative design.
3. Both experts and users were jointly involved in development. Experts were dominant in the early stages, users were dominant in the later stages.
4. Great attention was paid to the user's job satisfaction and to ensuring that the expert system increased this.

Mumford claims that the result was a non-threatening system which saved money for the company and which everyone liked to use.

11.11 CONCLUSION

Our main emphasis in this work has been to describe some of the contemporary conclusions surrounding the knowledge analysis stage of expert systems and expert database systems development. Wherever possible, we have also indicated how the adaptation of conventional anslysis techniques is feasible. This does not mean that considered design, implementation, evaluation and maintenance are not crucial to the success of an expert system or expert database system project. The literature on these activities is, however, not as well developed as that available for knowledge analysis.

11.12 RECALL EXERCISES

1. If five objects each having four possible values each feed into a knowledge module, what are the maximum number of production rules we will need?
2. If one object having three possible values outputs, what is the likely minimum number of rules we shall need?
3. How do we turn a decision tree into a rule set?
4. How do we turn an object dictionary into a set of frames?
5. Discuss some of the benefits of implementing a rule set as a relational database.
6. Distinguish between verification, validation and usability.
7. What is the most common method of testing expert systems and what are its disadvantages?
8. Discuss some of the problems involved in amending a knowledge base.
9. In what way does a technique such as determinancy diagramming ease the maintenance process?

11.13 OPEN-ENDED EXERCISES

1. Athanasiou has portrayed AI developments as an attempt to push the automation of the ideas of scientific management from the domain of physical and administrative work to the domain of intellectual work. Discuss this in the context of the human problems of expert system development.
2. Much of the literature describes rule base development as a mere accretion of rules. Design is not seen to be the issue. Discuss some of the problems that might be associated with this attitude, particularly for large-scale development.
3. Is knowledge base systems maintenance any easier than conventional systems maintenance?
4. Is a form of evaluation based around a set of test cases provided by the domain expert sufficient for commercial expert systems?

REFERENCES

Arbanel R.M. and Williams M.D. (1987). A relational representation for knowledge bases. In Kerschberg L. (Ed.) *Expert Database Systems*. Benjamin Cummings, New York.
Berry D.C. and Hart A. (1990). Evaluating expert systems. *Expert Systems*, 7(4), 199–207.
Bloomfield P.B. (1986). Capturing expertise by rule induction. *Knowledge Engineering Review*, 1(4), 55–67.
Mumford E. (1985). *Knowledge Engineering, Expert Systems and Organizational Change*. Working paper, Manchester Business School.
Preece A.D. (1990). Towards a methodology for evaluating expert systems. *Expert Systems*, 7(4), 215–223.
Suen C., Grogono P., Shinghal R. and Coallier F. (1990). Verifying, validating and measuring performance of expert systems. *Expert System with Applications*, 1(2), 93–102.
Yourdon E. and Constantine L.L. (1977). *Structured Design*, 2nd Edn. Yourdon Press, New York.

12

CONCLUSION

12.1 INTRODUCTION

Prediction is not a systematic science. Any attempt to predict the future by extrapolating from present trends is unlikely to be extremely accurate. Nevertheless, it is important to close this book with some indication of the likely short-term future of knowledge engineering, even if this largely reflects the hopes and aspirations of the author.

The main premise of this concluding chapter is that knowledge engineering, the discipline devoted to building knowledge base systems, will have an important effect on the whole process of developing the commercial information systems of the future. In this sense, we discuss the strategic importance of knowledge base systems along the conventional dimensions of the applications market: the vertical dimension and the horizontal dimension.

12.2 CRITIQUE OF AI

First, however, a note of caution. At the start of the author's introductory work on expert database systems (Beynon-Davies, 1991), the following quote was presented:

> Some people believe Artificial Intelligence is the most exciting scientific and commercial enterprise of the century. Others raise distress flags, fearing eventual misuse. Still others scoff, arguing that the technology will come to nothing. One thing is clear however: Artificial Intelligence generates passion, and passion stimulates hyperbole-riddled rhetoric, and that rhetoric dangerously obfuscates. It is hard to tell if the field's promoters are pied-pipers leading us to the disappointment of excessive expectations or missionaries beckoning us to an almost inconceivable opportunity. (Winston and Prendergast, 1984)

The general tone of the work on expert database systems was supportive of AI. AI was seen as an area of exciting promise, particularly in terms of developments in the integration of AI and database technology.

In recent years, however, a growing body of literature has developed supporting a less-flattering conception of AI. AI is seen as a large white elephant doomed to eventual failure. We shall collectively call this body of literature, primarily written by philosophers but also made up of contributions from at least two disaffected AI people, the *critique of AI* (Weizenbaum, 1976; Dreyfus, 1979; Searle, 1986; Winograd and Flores, 1986).

The critique of AI has quite clearly been fuelled by some excessive claims made by notable personalities in the field (McCorduck, 1978). For instance:

1. Newell and Simon's claim that intelligence is merely a matter of physical symbol manipulation.
2. John McCarthy's claim that even machines as simple as thermostats can be said to have beliefs.
3. Marvin Minsky's statement that the next generation of computer systems will be so intelligent that we will be lucky if they are willing to keep us around as household pets.

Our aim in this section is to introduce the basic elements of this critique and in particular to examine some of the consequences for knowledge engineering. We shall primarily use the work of Winograd and Flores (1986) to act as a backbone for the discussion.

The critique is based around a number of central premises:

1. AI is based on a limited ontology or theory of reality. AI follows the rationalistic tradition in assuming that:
   (a) there is an objective real-world;
   (b) we can characterize this real-world in terms of identifiable objects with well-defined properties;
   (c) we can find general rules that apply to situations in terms of these objects and properties;
   (d) applying such rules to the situation of concern we can draw valid conclusions.
2. AI uses a model of human cognition in which an agent manipulates mental representations.
3. AI assumes that such representations modelled on a computer can be portrayed as accurate models of human knowledge and intelligence.
4. The rationalistic tradition is a naive and simple ontology.
5. A more satisfactory ontology is to be found in the hermeneutic tradition, which assumes that:
   (a) reality is necessarily subjective. Objects and properties are not inherent in the world;
   (b) reality is founded in human interpretation and that all interpretation is based on prejudice which includes the assumptions implicit in the language a person uses;
   (c) we do not relate to things primarily through having representations of them;
   (d) meaning is fundamentally social and cannot be reduced to the meaning-giving activity of individual subjects.

6. AI as presently constituted is impossible.
7. The most productive future use of computers is as convivial tools for cooperative work.

In summary, since reality is a social construction, and what we mean by human intelligence and understanding is always determined by social context and background, programs that attempt to emulate these properties are always likely to be fundamentally flawed.

However, the view of expert systems provided by the critique is a little more forgiving than its view of AI in general. Winograd and Flores, for instance, make the observation that most expert systems do not try to deal with the difficult questions of relevance, context and background that bedevil the majority of programs in AI. As such, to the extent that domains can be well-defined and rules set down for them precisely, they expect such systems to continue proliferating and operate successfully. Along with Dreyfus, however, they take issue with the label *expert system*. They believe that calling a program *expert* is misleading in the same way as calling it *intelligent* or saying it *understands*. They also believe that in areas where background and context are extremely important, such as in many areas of medicine, the application of such systems is inherently limited.

One might be tempted, in view of the many cogent arguments presented by the critique, to write off AI as a scientific and commercial endeavour. However, this would be somewhat premature. It would be to deny many of the achievements of AI in directing developments in newer breeds of software.

The critique of AI exemplified by Winograd and Flores' work is primarily directed at what we might call 'hard' AI. Hard AI is directed at modelling human cognitive processes through simulation founded in symbolic representation and processing. In a sense, academics like Winograd and Flores are right in resurrecting a more philosophical and social conception of knowledge. Much of research in AI has worked within the remits of a naive philosophy, particularly a naive epistemology (see the working definition of knowledge given in Chapter 1).

However, the present work is supportive of what we might call 'soft' AI. In this conception, AI is seen as a breeding ground for newer forms of software. The aim is to build higher-level tools for software production. No claim is made as to the software replicating or simulating human intellect. The aim is to build more adaptable software that can augment the human intellect.

One of the most interesting proposals for such newer types of software is the concept of a norm-base (Stamper *et al.* 1991). The objective of a norm-base is to decouple the technical and organizational knowledge that is inextricably linked in contemporary application systems. The underlying principle is to find a way of specifying a social system as a system of norms, and from such a system to develop a working application system amenable to change.

12.3 COMMERCIAL ACCEPTANCE

Expert systems are presently a commercial proposition. They will become more so in the future. Indeed, what will probably happen is that the present divide between conventional software and software built using knowledge base principles will gradually fade. For instance, knowledge base software is already being embedded within conventional information systems to interface with databases.

The primary emphasis of this book has been to try to cast knowledge engineering as something which is not radically different from conventional information system practice. If it were radically different, involving something like a paradigmatic shift, then it would be unlikely that knowledge engineering would find a feasible commercial niche in the next decade. Because, however, knowledge engineering is better seen as an extension of conventional information systems development, the process of assimilation, particularly into the commercial world, should continue at a steady pace.

In the horizontal dimension, expert systems and expert database systems have an enormous scope for application within conventional information systems. Knowledge base systems have an important role to play in many traditional areas of business. For example:

1. Sales and order entry
2. Stock control and warehousing
3. Credit control
4. Management information
5. Business planning
6. Production scheduling
7. Manpower planning
8. Finance

In the vertical dimension, knowledge base technology has an important role to play in the CAISE tools of tomorrow. Contemporary computer-aided information systems engineering (CAISE) tools attempt to increase the productivity of information systems builders via graphical interfaces, cross-checking of systems, and automation of much of the task of systems documentation. Such tools are largely the result of the automation of well-established structured analysis and design techniques. However, existing CAISE technology does not address the fundamental characteristic of design. Design is a knowledge-intensive activity.

Knowledge base information systems engineering is likely to replace contemporary database information systems engineering. The current crop of database tools such as data dictionaries will be supplanted by knowledge base tools.

One of the most interesting application areas that crosses both the horizontal and vertical dimensions of application development is what we shall call the knowledge centre (Keller, 1987). The knowledge centre is a possible extension of the contemporary information centre concept. The information centre is a central facility within a company that supports a wide variety of tools and applications through which end-users can conduct useful work. Typically, today's information centre consists of a handful of poorly integrated database systems for report writing, decision support, graphics, statistical analysis and similar functions. Some companies are already investing in expert system interfaces that help users in manipulating corporate data and advise users as to the appropriate tool for the job they require.

12.4 BUILDING A FUTURE COMMERCIAL APPLICATION

The change in technology described above is likely to mean that the methods of building information systems will change. It is likely that a major part of what we now know as an information system will be constructed from a mixture of database and knowledge base components. Figure 12.1 is meant to illustrate the possibilities for information systems development in the short- to medium-term future. The system we assume is in use by a US national hotel chain.

Relational databases are probably likely to remain at the heart of the information systems effort, if only because they have proven extremely flexible tools for data management. Large corporate databases, probably distributed over a number of geographical sites, will be the norm. Hence, the subset of such a database – the hotels and rooms relations – displayed in the figure is likely to be fragmented in terms of the distribution of the organization's hotels in the US.

Semantic extensions to the relational model, perhaps based on the object-oriented declaration of domains, will certainly have a part to play. In our example, we have declared one of the columns of the Rooms table to be a complex graphic data type. Accessing this column will allow customers to select a room based on the view it has of the surrounding countryside or cityscape.

Most DBMS of the near future will offer knowledge management modules. Such modules will be primarily used to enforce data integrity. Integrity constraints, expressed probably in logic-based extensions to the SQL database sub-language, will enforce such issues as ensuring that no hotel is overbooked. Knowledge management modules will

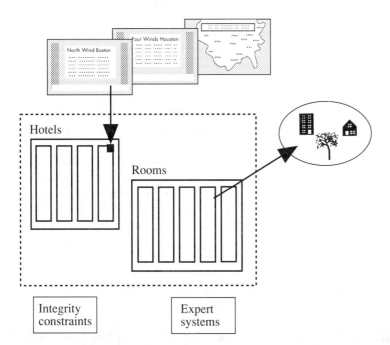

Figure 12.1   A possible commercial application (for a hotel chain) of a future information system.

also be used in a proactive sense, however, much in the way we currently interface expert systems to database systems. An expert system might be built for the hotels chain, for instance, that continually monitors bookings and suggests critical areas where intensive marketing is needed.

User interfaces are almost certainly going to be multimedia in flavour. We can expect graphics, sound and video to be important parts of future information systems. Customers will make an advanced booking at a hotel by first selecting a given hotel from a map of the US, then selecting a length of stay from an animated representation of a calendar, and finally selecting a given available room via selection from a three-dimensional map of the hotel.

12.5 STRATEGIC KNOWLEDGE PLANNING

A great deal of literature has built up around the use of information systems as a corporate resource (Earl, 1989). Most of this literature is directed at applying database technology to the task of strategic decision-making. Knowledge is a more encompassing concept than data (see Chapters 2 and 3). The sum total of the knowledge existing in an organization needs to be recognized as a major corporate resource.

Beerel suggests that managers should encourage the development and maintenance of knowledge banks based on workers' knowledge of markets, customers, products, competitors, the use of resources, etc. (Beerel, 1987). Such knowledge banks will drive the strategic information systems of the organization.

Expert systems, like database systems, are seen as a major means for an organization to gain competitive advantage. Competitive advantage comes in three forms:

1. Cost advantage. Areas involved in improving overall efficiency via better planning.
2. Differentiation. Aspects such as improving quality and reliability relative to price, better market understanding, image promotion, etc.
3. Location. Placing distribution, marketing and information outlets where required.

Any organization needs to identify areas in which it has relative superiority, and to use that superiority both to create barriers to entry as well as to launch strategic offensives. One popular method of doing this is the critical success factor concept (CSF). A CSF is a factor which is deemed crucial to the success of a business. CSFs are those areas that must be given special attention by management. They also represent critical points of leverage for achieving competitive advantage. The CSF for a chain of high street jewellers is likely to be location of its outlets; the CSF for a health authority is likely to be the quality or standard of service it gives to its customers, the patients.

CSFs are usually contrasted with CFFs, or critical failure factors. A CFF is an aspect of the organization, the poor management of which is likely to precipitate organizational failure. The CFF for the high street jeweller chain is likely to be a high amount of shrinkage in consumer demand. The CFF for a health authority might be poor coordination of its staff, particularly sub-contracted staff.

CSFs and CFFs are useful ways of identifying areas for the maximal application of expert systems. The high street jeweller chain would benefit from a system that selects optimal locations based on factors such as population density, state of local economy, etc. The health authority would benefit from a system which ensures the efficient scheduling of cleaning or the optimal use of catering services.

Another framework for assessing competitive advantage is proposed by Sviokla (1986) based on the work of Porter (1985). He argues that a successful firm shapes the structure of competition by influencing five primary forces: barriers to entry, threat of substitution, buyer bargaining power, supplier bargaining power, and industrial rivalry. Many combinations of these factors, such as low industrial rivalry, high barriers to entry, and low buyer bargaining power, can lead to sustainable, above-average, long-term profits.

The use of expert systems can clearly affect each of these five factors. For instance, increased industrial rivalry has resulted from a surge of activity in the area of expert systems for financial planning. Such systems have made it economically feasible to generate more complex financial plans for individuals of lower income. These same expert systems are likely to lower barriers of entry to the financial planning industry.

12.6 EXTENDING THE PENSION SYSTEM

To place this discussion in context let us refer to the Cymro case study again.

Probably the most critical success factor for the Cymro building society is the quality and quantity of services it can offer its customers. Our immediate aim therefore is to increase the business usefulness of the current pension system. Below we suggest a number of ways in which the pension system might be extended:

1. Data entry screen. Most current expert systems prompt the user for data a step at a time. This is primarily because such systems work in backward-chaining mode. A more satisfactory interface for the pension system might be provided via a forward-chaining system. In other words, the system would comprise a data entry screen that emulates the manual customer information form. Once the user has completed the form, the system inferences and produces a recommendation.
2. Customer records. Data collected by the system would prove invaluable for other purposes. It would therefore seem sensible to write the information, including the recommendation given by the system, to a database of customer records for further use.
3. Producing quotations. The present standalone quotation system might be included within the expert system itself. This might lead to easier maintenance.
4. Computerized input. Rather than collating the information from manual information forms, branches might be required to enter the information onto disk via local PCs and transmit the information to the central pensions facility. An alternative is to supply a copy of the system to each branch to run for themselves.
5. Standard letters. The database discussed in 2 above might be used in a number of different ways by Cymro. One of the most straightforward would be to produce standard letters.

12.6.1 Extending the system into a complete investment advisor

Perhaps the most radical extension of the system would be to make it merely a part of a

Figure 12.2   The relationship between advisors and customers at Cymro.

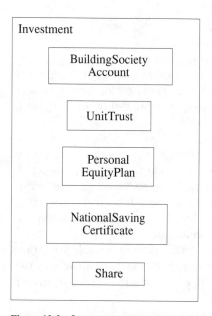

Figure 12.3   Investment types.

much larger knowledge base system. Such a system would constitute a complete investment advisor. Our overall aim in building such a system is to improve the investment service to the customer.

Cymro employs at least one person per branch known as a financial advisor. This person's remit is to offer financial advice to customers, of which investment advice is by far the largest part. The E–R diagram in Fig. 12.2 illustrates the relationship between advisors and customers.

Personal pensions are only one type of investment. Investment is clearly an object which constitutes a super-class. Contained within this object are clearly a number of

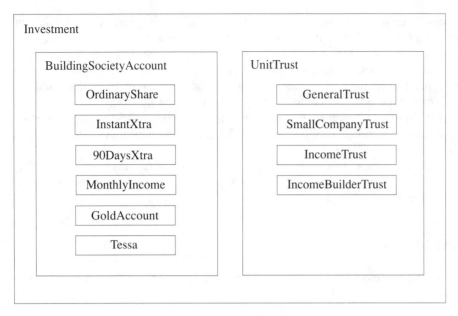

Figure 12.4   Accounts and unit trusts offered by Cymro.

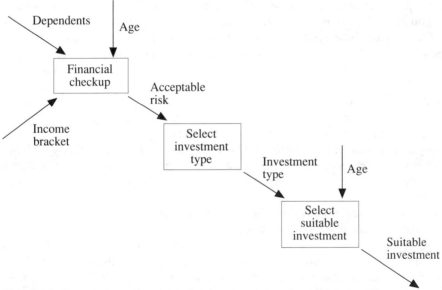

Figure 12.5   Process of matching appropriate investments to a given customer profile.

investment types such as building society accounts, unit trusts, personal equity plans (PEPs), etc. Some such types are illustrated as an E–R diagram in Fig. 12.3. We can, of course, continue this decomposition to at least one more level. Hence, Fig. 12.4 illustrates a series of actual building society accounts and unit trusts offered by Cymro.

The expertise involved in the role of advisor amounts to selecting a range of appropriate investments that match a given customer's profile. We might therefore define financial advice as a three-step iterative process. In the first step, which we call the financial checkup, we build a customer profile. In the second step, we select a suitable investment type. In the third step, we select a specific investment from the portfolio offered by Cymro. Figure 12.5 documents this process as a data-flow diagram.

This diagram indicates how a range of linked expert systems would need to be built. One for producing a customer profile, one for selecting investment types, and one each for a specific type of investment.

We would expect such a system to improve the leverage of Cymro in its market. Its ability to offer up-to-date, on-the-spot, extensive planning to its customers is likely to improve its market share, at least in the short term.

12.7 CONCLUSION

We summarize here some of the major conclusions of this work and reference them to chapters:

1. The main aim of the work has been to propose a framework for synthesizing the methods, tools and techniques of knowledge engineering with the methods, tools and techniques of conventional information systems work. The framework is initially founded on an analysis of information and information systems and consequently the place of knowledge base systems within organizations. It is suggested that characterizing knowledge base systems as semi-formal information systems offers a useful means for identifying knowledge base projects for competitive advantage (Chapter 2).

2. Knowledge representation is a central issue in computing. Knowledge representation is not the sole prerogative of AI or knowledge engineering. It is of equal relevance to conventional information systems work (Chapter 3).

3. Knowledge engineering has traditionally been identified almost exclusively with the development of expert systems. We prefer a larger definition of the term that allows scope to encompass the convergence between areas such as AI and database work (Chapter 4).

4. The convergence in technology described in Beynon-Davies (1991) must be met with a parallel convergence in methodology (Chapter 5).

5. Knowledge base systems are presently a commercial proposition and are likely to become more so in the future. In making the transition from the academic to the commercial world, suitable problem–method connections have to be identified. In particular, a suitable compromise must be made between a structured and a prototyping approach to knowledge base development (Chapter 5).

6. A number of methodologies for knowledge base systems development have been proposed over the last decade or so. KADS is probably one of the most prominent in Eupope (Chapter 5).

7. Expert systems and expert database systems are best seen as mechanisms for extending the boundaries of conventional information systems. Standard information systems work within the formal or structured domain of organizations. Expert

database systems offer potential in the semi-formal or unstructured domain of organizations (Chapter 6).

8. The nature of expert systems and knowledge engineering changes subtly with this change of application. Much of the expertise embodied in expert database systems is not high-level knowledge held by one 'star' domain expert. Corporate knowledge is more likely to represent low-level knowledge distributed throughout an organization (Chapters 6 and 7).

9. Knowledge analysis is the stage which most clearly distinguishes knowledge base systems development from conventional systems development. Knowledge elicitation or acquisition is a far more intensive process than conventional systems analysis (Chapter 7).

10. No one methodology offers the entire solution to building knowledge base systems. This work has therefore discussed a range of techniques that might contribute to the working toolkit of the knowledge engineer (Chapter 8).

11. Many information systems analysis and design techniques may be adapted to the exigencies of knowledge engineering, thereby encouraging the process of convergence. Some techniques are directed at driving the process of knowledge elicitation (Chapter 8). Others are directed at documenting the results of elicitation (Chapter 9).

12. Conventional data-oriented techniques, such as E–R and dependency diagramming, can be adapted to the needs of documenting structural knowledge (Chapter 9).

13. Conventional process-oriented techniques, such as data-flow diagramming and decision trees, can be adapted to the needs of documenting behavioural knowledge (Chapter 9).

14. An approach based in object-oriented analysis offers some hope in providing an integrated method for documenting both structural and behavioural knowledge (Chapter 10).

15. Knowledge base systems can be implemented in many distinct ways. We have particularly contrasted representation in classic representation formalisms, such as production rules, with some of the developing enhanced architectures for database systems (Chapter 11).

16. Issues of evaluation, testing and maintenance are of equal relevance to knowledge base systems as they are to conventional systems (Chapter 11).

17. Knowledge base systems work, as exemplified by 'hard' AI, has been built on a naive epistemology. A conception of 'soft' AI is more appropriate for commercial exploitation (Chapter 12).

18. Corporate knowledge is likely to be seen as a logical development from corporate data, particularly in its ability to provide competitive advantage (Chapter 12). The main benefits of expert database systems usually result from the codification, maintenance and dissemination of valuable corporate knowledge.

12.8 RECALL EXERCISES

1. Discuss the basis on which the critique of AI is based.
2. Does the critique mean the end of knowledge engineering?
3. What is the knowledge centre?

4. What is a critical success factor and how does it apply to knowledge engineering?
5. Discuss in what way expert systems can usefully contribute to information systems.

12.9 OPEN-ENDED EXERCISES

1. Pick up a leaflet on some aspect of government or organizational legislation (e.g. social security entitlement, personal tax allowances, VAT calculation, entitlement to travelling expenses, etc.). Analyse the knowledge contained therein and design an expert system based on this analysis.
2. For the application in 1, identify appropriate connections to corporate data.
3. Ben-David and Sterling (1986) claim the following benefits for financial expert systems:
   (a) A combination of human experts with a good expert system can lead to better decision-making.
   (b) A good system can help in the reduction of bureaucratic processes in banking institutions and can also increase the control of management over the organization.
   (c) The time spent on trivial and straightforward cases can be lessened.
   (d) The service to customers can be improved by shortening the turnaround of requests.
   Discuss each of these held benefits in the light of the Cymro case study.

REFERENCES

Ben-David A. and Sterling L. (1986). A prototype expert system for credit evaluation. In Pau L.F. (Ed.). *Artificial Intelligence in Economics and Management*. North-Holland, Amsterdam.
Beynon-Davies P. (1991). *Expert Database Systems: A Gentle Introduction*. McGraw-Hill, London.
Beerel A.C. (1987). *Expert Systems: Strategic Implications and Applications*. Ellis Horwood, Chichester.
Dreyfus H.L. (1979). *What Computers Can't Do: A Critique of Artificial Reason*. Harper and Row, New York.
Earl M.J. (1989). *Management Strategies for Information Technology*. Prentice-Hall, Hemel Hempstead.
Keller R. (1987). *Expert System Technology – Development and Application*. Yourdon Press, New York.
McCorduck P. (1978). *Machines Who Think*. Freeman and Co, New York.
Porter M.E. (1985). *Competitive Advantage: Creating and Sustaining Superior Performance*. Free Press, New York.
Searle J.R. (1986). *Minds, Brains and Science*. Harvard University Press.
Stamper R., Liu K., Kolkman M., Klarenberg P., Van Slooten F., Ades Y. and Van Slooten C. (1991). From database to normbase. *International Journal of Information Management*, 11 (1), 67–84.
Sviokla J. (1986). Business implications of knowledge-based systems. *Database*, Summer and Fall.
Weizenbaum J. (1976). *Computer Power and Human Reason*. Freeman and Co, New York.
Winograd T. and Flores F. (1986). *Understanding Computers and Cognition: A New Foundation for Design*. Ablex Publishing, Norwood, NJ.
Winston P.H. and Prendergast K.A. (Eds.) (1984). *The AI Business: the Commercial Uses of Artificial Intelligence*. MIT Press, Boston, MA.

A LEVEL5 KNOWLEDGE BASE

In this appendix we illustrate how the personal pension selection system looks in the syntax of a commercially available expert system shell. The shell is Level5, available from Information Builders. Below we list the pension knowledge base that would be stored first in a .PRL and then compiled into a .KNB file. The lines beginning with an exclamation mark represent explanatory comments.

TITLE Personal Pension Selection System DISPLAY

PERSONAL PENSION SELECTION SYSTEM

This system recommends one of the current personal plans offered by the CYMRO building society on the basis of a profile of the customer.

****Please click on <continue>****

!This section provides a documentary title for the system and
!an initial startup screen.

ATTRIBUTE employmentStatus
AND security
AND recommendation
AND sex

NUMERIC contributionPeriod
AND age
AND preferredRetirementAge

!Facts have to be typed in Level5. Simple strings (simplefacts)
!such as 'employee is in serps' do not have to be declared.
!Attribute facts store alphanumeric values. Numeric facts store numbers

1. system is complete DISPLAY shutdown

!This sets up the simplefact for the system to solve and identifies the
!closedown screen

RULE control rule
IF contribution details
AND recommendation IS amicable
OR recommendation IS prudent
OR recommendation IS equitable
OR recommendation IS premiumAccount
OR recommendation IS checkDetails
OR recommendation IS stayInScheme
THEN system is complete

!This is the top-most rule used merely to sequence the process of
!calculating contribution details before producing a recommendation

RULE contribution details 1
IF age < 65
AND sex IS male
AND preferredRetirementAge = 0
THEN contribution details
AND contributionPeriod := 65 − age

RULE contribution details 2
IF age < 65
AND sex IS female
AND preferredRetirementAge = 0
THEN contribution details
AND contributionPeriod := 60 − age

RULE contribution details 3
IF age < 65
AND sex IS male
AND preferredRetirementAge > 0
THEN contribution details
AND contributionPeriod := preferredRetirementAge − age

RULE contribution details 4
IF age < 65
AND sex IS female
AND preferredRetirementAge > 0
THEN contribution details
AND contributionPeriod := preferredRetirementAge − age

!Rules 1 to 4 calculate the appropriate contribution period for
!the customer. Note how the calculation has to be specified as the
!second conclusion of a rule. Level5 prohibits the first conclusion
!from being a numeric fact.

RULE selfEmployed 1
IF employmentStatus IS selfEmployed
AND contributionPeriod > 10
THEN recommendation IS amicable

RULE selfEmployed 2
IF employmentStatus IS selfEmployed
AND contributionPeriod $\leq$ 10
THEN recommendation IS premiumAccount

!The two rules above recommend for self employed customers

RULE Employed 1
IF employmentStatus IS employed
AND employee is in a company scheme
AND employee is in serps
THEN recommendation IS premiumAccount

RULE Employed 2
IF employmentStatus IS employed
And employee is in a company scheme
AND NOT employee is in serps
THEN recommendation IS stayInScheme

RULE Employed 3
IF employmentStatus IS employed
AND NOT employee is in a company scheme
AND NOT employee is in serps
THEN recommendation IS checkDetails

RULE Employed 4
IF employmentStatus IS employed
AND NOT employee is in a company scheme
AND employee is in serps
AND contributionPeriod $>$ 25
THEN recommendation IS equitable

RULE Employed 5
IF employmentStatus IS employed
AND NOT employee is in a company scheme
AND employee is in serps
AND contributionPeriod $\leq$ 25
AND contributionPeriod $\geq$ 22
AND security IS high
THEN recommendation IS equitable

RULE Employed 6
IF employmentStatus IS employed
AND NOT employee is in a company scheme
AND employee is in serps
AND contributionPeriod $\leq$ 25
AND contributionPeriod $\geq$ 22
AND security IS low
THEN recommendation IS prudent

RULE Employed 7
IF employmentStatus IS employed
AND NOT employee is in a company scheme
AND employee is in serps
AND contributionPeriod $\leq$ 25
AND contributionPeriod $\geq$ 22

AND security IS dontKnow
THEN recommendation IS equitable

RULE Employed 8
IF employmentStatus IS employed
AND NOT employee is in a company scheme
AND employee is in serps
AND contributionPeriod < 22
AND contributionPeriod ⩾ 10
THEN recommendation IS prudent

RULE Employed 9
IF employmentStatus IS employed
AND NOT employee is in a company scheme
AND employee is in serps
AND contributionPeriod < 10
THEN recommendation IS premiumAccount

!The rules above recommend for employed customers

TEXT employmentStatus
How would you describe the employment status of the customer?

TEXT age
Give me the current age of the customer.

TEXT sex
Is the customer male or female?

TEXT preferredRetirement Age
At what age does the customer wish to retire?
(Enter 0 if unknown or if statutory retirement age)

TEXT security
How would you best describe the amount of security required by the customer?

!The TEXT command allows us to customize the default prompt associated
!with questions

DISPLAY shutdown

We recommend the following:

[recommendation]

!The DISPLAY command forces a message to the screen. In this case
!we are making an indirect call to the value of recommendation.

A LEONARDO KNOWLEDGE BASE

In this appendix we illustrate how the personal pension selection system looks in the syntax of the LEONARDO expert system shell. This shell is interesting as an example of a hybrid of production rules and frames. Originally a product of Creative Logic, it is now available from Brenda Management Services (BMS).

First we list the simple version of the knowledge base which expects the user to input the appropriate contribution period directly. Comments are lines beginning with the characters /*.

SEEK recommendation

/* All LEONARDO knowledge bases must have a SEEK. This sets the goal object for the system.

IF employmentStatus is selfEmployed
AND contributionPeriod > 10
THEN recommendation is amicable

IF employmentStatus is selfEmployed
AND contributionPeriod ≤ 10
THEN recommendation is premiumAccount

IF employmentStatus is employed
AND companyScheme is yes
AND serps is yes
THEN recommendation is premiumAccount

IF employmentStatus is employed
AND companyScheme is yes
AND serps is no
THEN recommendation is stayInScheme

IF employmentStatus is employed
AND companyScheme is no
AND serps is no
THEN recommendation is checkDetails

IF employmentStatus is employed
AND companyScheme is no
AND serps is yes
AND contributionPeriod $\geq$ 25
THEN recommendation is equitable

IF employmentStatus is employed
AND companyScheme is no
AND serps is yes
AND contributionPeriod $<$ 25
AND contributionPeriod $\geq$ 22
AND security is high
THEN recommendation is equitable

IF employmentStatus is employed
AND companyScheme is no
AND serps is yes
AND contributionPeriod $<$ 25
AND contributionPeriod $\geq$ 22
AND security is low
THEN recommendation is prudent

IF employmentStatus is employed
AND companyScheme is no
AND serps is yes
AND contributionPeriod $<$ 25
AND contributionPeriod $\geq$ 22
AND security is unknown
THEN recommendation is prudent

IF employmentStatus is employed
AND companyScheme is no
AND serps is yes
AND contributionPeriod $<$ 22
AND contributionPeriod $\geq$ 10
THEN recommendation is prudent

IF employmentStatus is employed
AND companyScheme is no
AND serps is yes
AND contributionPeriod $<$ 10
THEN recommendation is premiumAccount

For each object in a rule base (any string on the left-hand side of a condition or conclusion), LEONARDO maintains a frame made up of a number of standard slots. The frame below illustrates how this frame is filled for the employmentStatus object:

```
        Name:   employmentStatus
    LongName:   current employment status
        Type:   text
       Value:
    Certainty:
 DerivedFrom:
 DefaultValue:   employed
  FixedValue:
AllowedValue:   employed, selfEmployed
ComputeValue:
     OnError:
 QueryPrompt:   Is the customer employed or selfEmployed?
 QueryPreface:   Employment Status of Customer
   Expansion:
  Commentary:
 Introduction:
  Conclusion:
```

The Name and Type slots are automatically created from detail in the rule base. Value, Certainty, and DerivedFrom are slots used by the system at run-time and cannot be accessed directly by the user. DefaultValue is the value that the object should take if the user answers unknown to a question about an object. The AllowedValue object stipulates the possible values for this object. The system at run-time will generate a picking list for the user. QueryPrompt tailors the prompt to the user. QueryPreface paints the top-half of a screen with explanatory text.

Object frames can also be declared for procedures attached to the rule base. Suppose, for instance, we wish to calculate a customer's contribution period from his or her age and sex. We might use the following rule base:

```
SEEK contributionCalculation

IF age > 0
AND preferredRetirementAge = 0
AND sex is male
THEN preferredRetirementAge = 65;
RUN getContributionPeriod(preferredRetirementAge, age, contributionPeriod);
task is complete

IF age > 0
AND preferredRetirementAge = 0
AND sex is female
THEN preferredRetirementAge = 60;
RUN getContributionPeriod(preferredRetirementAge, age, contributionPeriod);
task is complete

IF age > 0
AND preferredRetirementAge > 0
THEN RUN getContributionPeriod(preferredRetirementAge, age, contributionPeriod);
task is complete
```

The RUN statement in each rule will access a procedure specified by the following frame:

```
        Name:   getContributionPeriod
    LongName:
        Type:   procedure
 AcceptsReal:   preferredRetirementAge, age
 AcceptsText:
 AcceptsList:
 ReturnsReal:   contributionPeriod
 ReturnsText:
 ReturnsList:
   LocalReal:
   LocalText:
   LocalList:
        Body:
contributionPeriod = preferredRetirementAge − age
```

The slots in this frame act much in the sense of header declarations of conventional procedural programs. We specify the input and output parameters to the procedure and any local variables used. The text following the body slot is expected to be in the syntax of LEONARDO's procedural programming language. Here we are conducting a simple calculation.

CHAPTER 1

1. The symbolic representation of some universe of discourse.
2. The discipline devoted to the simulation of human cognitive processes.
3. The discipline devoted to building knowledge base systems.
4. An expert system that makes no connection to other files or software.
5. A delimited area of knowledge.
6. Knowledge elicitation is the process of extracting the knowledge relevant to some domain. Knowledge representation is the process of mapping this knowledge onto a computational medium.
7. A knowledge engineer is a specialist in building knowledge base systems. A domain expert is a person skilled in a particular knowledge domain.
8. A first order knowledge base system is one built by connecting together diverse technology such as expert system shells and DBMS. A second order knowledge base system is built using one consistent architecture.
9. Expert systems are a subset of the set of knowledge base systems.
10. The movement from standalone expert systems to interconnected knowledge base systems.

CHAPTER 2

1. An increment of knowledge which can be inferred from data.
2. The purpose of an information system is to support a human activity system. The purpose of an information system is to serve real-world action.

3. Semiotics is the study of signs. Information systems are systems of signs.
4. Technical information systems are primarily computerized information systems. Formal information systems are systems of rules and regulations. Informal information systems are systems of conventions, norms, values and beliefs.
5. They bridge the boundary of the formal and informal domains.

CHAPTER 3

1. An architecture for data.
2. Relational database is a formalism for fact bases.
3. A data model incorporating increased semantic content.
4. An IF-THEN rule. A knowledge representation formalism popular in expert systems work.
5. IF age $\geq$ 35 AND age $\leq$ 50 THEN ageCategory is middleAged
   IF ageCategory is middleAged THEN temperament is likely cautious
   IF temperament is likely cautious THEN preference is safeInvestment
6. A knowledge representation formalism designed to represent packets of knowledge.
7. Name: age
   Description: person's age
   Type: numeric
   Values: 1–100
   Default:

   Name: ageCategory
   Description: seven ages of man
   Type: text
   Values: infant, child, teenager, adult, middle-aged, elderly, dead
   Default: adult

   Name: temperament
   Description: the general personality of caution
   Type: text
   Values: cautious, adventurous
   Default: cautious

   Name: preference
   Description: investment preference
   Type: text
   Values: safeInvestment, riskInvestment
   Default: safeInvestment

8. Forward chaining is data-directed inference. Rules are driven by matching facts against the IF parts of rules. Backward chaining is goal-directed reasoning. Rules are driven by matching against the THEN parts of rules.
9. Facts are relationships between objects. Information is facts plus interpretation (meaning). Rules are mechanisms for generating new facts.

10. The process of applying facts and rules to generate new facts.
11. The first statement relates an object to its attribute and value. The second statement relates an object to an object class.
12. The process of transferring properties from high-level object classes to lower-level object classes or instances.

CHAPTER 4

1. To replicate or simulate the expertise in some domain.
2. Skilled performance or competence in some domain.
3. Interpretation, prediction, diagnosis, repair.
4. A shell is an expert system without the domain-specific knowledge.
5. A term used normally to refer to the enhancement of expert system technology with database facilities or vice versa.
6. Advantages: low cost; good for experimentation.
   Disadvantages: limited representation formalisms; lack of access to corporate data.
7. To increase access to large corporate fact bases.
8. Ensuring that a database remains a true reflection of the world it models. Integrity is about business rules.
9. Expertise becomes low-level, distributed, corporate knowledge.

CHAPTER 5

1. Identifying the key concepts and relationships in a particular domain.
2. Elicit–build/refine–evaluate iterative process.
3. Advantages: good for eliciting knowledge. Disadvantages: may lead to a disorganized system.
4. Knowledge engineering is a white elephant doomed to eventual failure.
5. Knowledge engineering offers a more encompassing solution to the software development problem than software engineering.
6. Structured development leads to well-organized, maintainable systems.
7. KADS is a framework for knowledge base development.
8. Seven stages – from knowledge analysis through to knowledge refinement. The analysis stage is the most heavily documented.

CHAPTER 6

1. Project selection is a loose-grained filter, designed to weed out the wheat from the chaff. The feasibility study is a close-grained filter, designed to weed out the bad wheat from the good wheat.
2. It involves the interaction of a series of criteria to come to some conclusion. A classic expert system application.
3. The business analysis approach involves the search for unstructured decision-making areas.

4. Can be tied to a corporate information systems planning effort.
5. Structured: calculating national insurance contributions; calculating sick pay; determining child benefit allowance. Unstructured: staff timetabling; producing a business plan; targeting a mail-shot.
6. The business analysis approach identifies fruitful areas. The checklist approach selects among alternatives.
7. They lie on the boundary of formal (structured) and informal (unstructured) decision-making.

CHAPTER 7

1. This depends on your point of view. Some people see acquisition as extraction from non-human knowledge sources. Elicitation is reserved for extraction from human knowledge sources.
2. Multiple knowledge engineers; multiple domain experts; dispersed knowledge.
3. That the more expert someone becomes, the less able they are to describe the principles of their expertise.
4. Manuals, literature, domain experts, videos, etc.
5. To validate each other.
6. Achieving some consensus model of expertise.
7. Interviews, observation, protocol analysis.
8. The process of inducing a rule set from a set of examples.
9. Advantages: elicitation may prove easier if a set of examples is available.
   Disadvantages: the rule set induced may not be the most organized one.

CHAPTER 8

1. A free-form representation for inter-connected concepts.
2. Identification of, and relationship between, concepts is made far more explicit.
3. In segments or in ripples.
4. A graphic technique for formally representing the knowledge contained in natural language statements.
5. A diagram of dependency relationships between attributes in some domain.
6. A directional one-to-one correspondence between the values of attributes.
7. Useful as a mechanism for driving elicitation and as a means for producing a redundancy-free knowledge base.
8. A general model of expertise relevant to specific domain-types.
9. A framework for considering the levels of knowledge associated with a particular domain.

CHAPTER 9

1. It encourages the process of integration between knowledge base systems and conventional systems.

2. A diagram of the things of interest and relationships between such things in some domain.
3. A representation of information flow. Useful for documenting procedural knowledge.
4. A tree-like representation of the relationship between decisions.
5. A method of specifying the objects pertinent to a domain.
6. Declarative knowledge is a framework for facts. Procedural knowledge implies frameworks for rules.

CHAPTER 10

1. Data-directed stream and process-directed stream.
2. An entity is a structural concept. An object displays both a structural and a behavioural aspect.
3. Entity models document structural or declarative knowledge. Object models document both declarative and procedural knowledge.
4. The binding together of data and procedures surrounded by a common interface.
5. A message is a communication between objects. A method is a procedure associated with objects.
6. Objects to relations; object ID to primary key; other attributes become non-key attributes; one-to-many relationships implemented via a foreign key; etc.
7. Overlapping subclasses.

CHAPTER 11

1. 20
2. 3
3. Each branch of the decision tree becomes a rule.
4. Each object definition becomes a frame.
5. Verification is determining whether a system meets its specification. Validation determines whether a system performs correctly. Usability generally refers to the interface aspects of the system.
6. Black-box testing. Difficult to debug such monolithic systems.
7. Dependencies between rules; overlapping rules; missing rules.
8. Reduces redundancy in a knowledge base.

CHAPTER 12

1. That 'hard' AI is based on a naive or simplistic concept of reality.
2. Knowledge engineering is based in 'soft' AI. Soft AI emphasizes the discipline's contribution in generating newer techniques for software production.
3. A development from the information centre concept. A facilitating department for corporate knowledge.
4. As mechanisms for extending the boundaries of useful computerization.

GLOSSARY

AKO
A-Kind-Of relationship between objects. Generalization link.

Alvey
A British programme of investment in information technology research produced in response to the Japanese fifth generation proposal.

Artificial intelligence
The discipline devoted to producing systems that perform tasks which would require 'intelligence' if performed by a human being.

Assertion
Otherwise known as a fact. A proposition whose validity is accepted.

Attribute
The property of an object.

Automatic knowledge acquisition
A branch of machine learning devoted to explicating the principles of the induction of rule bases.

Automatic knowledge acquisition facility
A facility available in some expert system shells and environments for producing a rule base from a set of examples.

Backtracking
The process of backing up through a series of inferences in the face of unacceptable results.

Backward chaining
An inference mechanism which works from a goal and attempts to satisfy a set of initial conditions. Also referred to as goal-directed chaining.

Class
See **Object class**

Conceptual graphs
A knowledge analysis technique based on the work on semantic net (Sowa).

Conceptual modelling
Before entering knowledge onto a computer it is necessary to construct a model of such knowledge and how it is used in terms of diagrams, etc. This is conceptual modelling.

Context diagram
The top-most data-flow diagram. Meant merely to orient the reader to the major interfaces of a system.

Data flow
A component of a data-flow diagram. A pipeline of data.

Data-flow diagram (DFD)
A process analysis technique. Designed to document the procedural nature of some information system.

Data model
An architecture for data.

Data store
A component of a data-flow diagram. A repository for data.

Database
A structured pool of data. A fact base.

Decision space
Also known as the problem space. The area that is defined by all the possible states that could occur as a result of the interactions between items in some domain.

Decision tree
A diagrammatic mechanism for representing heavily-nested structured decision-making.

Declarative knowledge
Forms of knowledge which make assertions about entities and the relationships between them.

Dependency
An association between data-items.

Dependency diagram
This technique is used normally to document the association between data-items as a preliminary step to producing a normalized database.

Determinancy
See **Dependency**

Determinancy diagram
See **Dependency diagram**

Direct method (elicitation)
A method for eliciting explicit knowledge – interviews, observation.

Domain
A bounded area of knowledge. A pool of values used to define columns of a relation.

Domain expert
The person who provides the expertise on which a knowledge base is modelled.

Encapsulation
The binding together of data and procedures in an object.

Entity
Some thing which has independent existence and can be uniquely identified.

Entity model
A model of a real-world domain expressed in terms of entities and relationships.

Entity–relationship data model
A data model due to P.P.S. Chen. Originally meant to be a competitor to the relational data model; now most commonly used as a conceptual modelling tool.

Entity–relationship diagram
A diagrammatic convention associated with the entity–relationship data model.

ESPRIT
A European Community-funded initiative in information technology research.

Expert database system
A system which marries the properties of database systems with the properties of expert systems.

Expert system
A computer system that achieves high levels of performance in areas that for human beings require large amounts of expertise.

Expert system shell
An expert system stripped of its domain-specific knowledge.

Expertise
The set of capabilities underlying skilled performance in some task area.

Explanation facility
The mechanisms for justifying or rationalizing the actions of a knowledge base system.

External entity
A component of a data-flow diagram. A net provider or receiver of system data.

Fact
A relationship between objects.

Foreign key
A column or group of columns of some relation that draws its values from the same domain as the primary key of another table.

Formal information system
Formal systems are systems of defined rules, regulations and procedures.

Forward chaining
An inference mechanism which works from a set of initial conditions to a goal. Also referred to as data-directed chaining.

Frame
A knowledge representation scheme that describes objects in terms of slots and fillers.

Generic model
A term used in KADS to describe the ideal–typical characteristics of problem-solving in some general knowledge domain.

Heuristic
A rule of thumb. A mechanism with no guarantee of success.

Hypermedia
A style of building information systems from loosely structured nodes of different media.

ID3
An algorithm developed by J.R. Quinlan for rule induction from a set of examples.

Indirect method (elicitation)
Techniques designed to elicit implicit knowledge by analysing tangential behaviours – multi-dimensional scaling, repertory grid analysis.

Inference
The process of generating conclusions from conditions or new facts from known facts.

Inference engine
That part of an expert system which makes inferences from the knowledge base.

Information engineering
A term used to refer to the set of inter-related disciplines needed to build a computerized enterprise based on data systems.

Informal information system
Informal information systems are characterized by norms, values and beliefs. Informal information systems provide the context for formal information systems.

Inheritance
The transference of properties from ancestor objects to descendent objects.

ISA
Is-instance-of relationship between objects and object classes.

Join
An operator of the relational algebra.

KADS
Knowledge Acquisition and Design System. One of the foremost European methodologies for expert system development.

Knowledge
The symbolic representation of some universe of discourse.

Knowledge acquisition
See **Knowledge elicitation**

Knowledge analysis
A stage in the expert system development life-cycle meant to encompass knowledge elicitation plus associated documentation.

Knowledge base
A collection of facts and rules which represent the knowledge in a particular domain.

Knowledge base management system (KBMS)
A management system for knowledge bases.

Knowledge base system (KBS)
A system containing knowledge which can perform tasks that require intelligence if done by human beings.

Knowledge elicitation
The process of locating, collecting and refining the knowledge relevant to a particular domain.

Knowledge engineer
A person, analagous to the systems analyst in traditional computing, who builds a KBS.

Knowledge representation
The process of mapping the knowledge of some domain into a computational medium.

Knowledge source
Any source for knowledge – documents, manuals, tape recordings, etc.

Levelling
The process of producing a hierarchically organized set of data-flow diagrams.

LISP
A functional language developed for list processing. The favoured language of the US AI community.

Message
A communication between objects.

Method
A behaviour associated with an object.

Multi-dimensional scaling
An indirect elicitation technique designed to plot discriminatory responses in a multi-dimensional space.

NIAM
Njissen's Information Analysis Method. An information system analysis technique popular in Scandinavia.

Object
Some aspect of the real world.

Object class
A category of objects.

Object diagram
A representation of the objects, attributes, relationships, methods and messages in some domain.

Object dictionary
A specification written in an extended version of Backus–Naur form.

Object identity
Every object must be uniquely identifiable. This is normally ensured via an object identifier.

Object model
A representation of the objects in some domain. Normally expressed as an object diagram.

Object-oriented analysis
A style of systems analysis based in the object-oriented paradigm.

Overview diagram
A DFD at level 1 of a hierarchy. Used to detail major processes and flows in an information system.

Primary key
A column or group of columns of a relation whose values are used to uniquely identify rows of a relation.

Process
A component of a DFD. A transformation of data flows.

Production rule
An IF-THEN rule having a set of conditions and a set of consequent conclusions.

Project
An operator of the relational algebra.

PROLOG
A logic programming language. The favoured language of much of the European AI community and the Japanese fifth generation project.

Protocol analysis
A knowledge acquisition technique which involves analysing a detailed record of an expert in action.

Relation
A disciplined table. The one data structure of the relational data model.

Relational algebra
The data manipulation part of the relational data model.

Relational data model
One of the most popular of the contemporary data models.

Repertory grid
A knowledge elicitation technique used to represent a person's view of the world in terms of personal constructs.

Rule
A mechanism for generating new facts.

Select
An operator of the relational algebra. The information retrieval command of SQL.

Semantic data model
A data model which attempts to provide a more expressive means of representing the meaning of information.

Semantic nets
A network which incorporates meaning. Taken originally from work undertaken in cognitive psychology.

Sink
See **External entity**

Shell
An expert system emptied of its domain-specific knowledge.

Slot
The major component of a frame.

Software engineering
The systematic application of an appropriate set of techniques to the whole process of software development.

Source
See **External entity**

Structured decision-making
The decision-making process can be described in detail before an actual decision is made.

Structured development
The process of developing systems via a series of well-defined steps, each step being defined in terms of the application of a given set of techniques in a determined sequence.

Structured Query Language (SQL)
The major database sub-language supporting the relational data model.

Spider diagram
A method of relating concepts together in a free-form way by lines.

Unstructured decision-making
The decision-making process cannot be described in detail. Driven by heuristics.

Working memory
A component of an expert system. A temporary store. A place for storing intermediate results.

REFERENCES AND FURTHER READING

Addis T.R. (1987). *Designing Knowledge Base Systems*. Kogan Page, London.

Alty J.L. and Coombs M.J. (1984). *Expert Systems: Concepts and Examples*. NCC Publications, Manchester.

Al-Zobaidie A. and Grimson J.B. (1987). Expert systems and database systems: how can they serve each other? *Expert Systems*, **4**(1), 30–37.

Anderson P.B. (1991). *A Theory of Computer Semiotics: Semiotic Approaches to the Construction and Assessment of Computer Systems*. Cambridge University Press, Cambridge.

Arbanel R.M. and Williams M.D. (1987). A relational representation for knowledge bases. In Kerschberg L. (Ed.) *Expert Database Systems*. Benjamin Cummings, New York.

Athanasiou T. (1985). Artificial intelligence: cleverly disguised politics. In Salomonides T. and Levidou L. *Compulsive Technology: Computers as Culture*. Free Association Books, New York.

Barr A. and Feigenbaum E. A. (1982). *The Handbook of Artificial Intelligence*. Vols 1, 2, 3. MIT Press, Boston, MA.

Barrett M.L. and Beerel A.C. (1988). *Expert Systems in Business: A Practical Approach*. Ellis Horwood, Chichester.

Beerel A.C. (1987). *Expert Systems: Strategic Implications and Applications*. Ellis Horwood, Chichester.

Berry D.C. and Hart A. (1990). Evaluating expert systems. *Expert Systems*, **7**(4), 199–207.

Beynon-Davies P. (1987). Software engineering and knowledge engineering: unhappy bedfellows? *Computer Bulletin*, December.

Beynon-Davies P. (1989). *Information Systems Development*. Macmillan, London.

Beynon-Davies P. (1991a). *Expert Database Systems: A Gentle Introduction*. McGraw-Hill, London.

Beynon-Davies P. (1991b). *Relational Database Systems: A Pragmatic Approach*. Blackwell Scientific, Oxford.

Beynon-Davies P. (to be published 1992). *Relational Database Design*. Blackwell Scientific, Oxford.

Blaha M.R., Premerlani W.J. and Rumbaugh J.E. (1988). Relational database design using an object-oriented methodology. *Comm. ACM*, **31**(4), 414–427.

Bloomfield P.B. (1986). Capturing expertise by rule induction. *Knowledge Engineering Review*, **1**(4), 55–67.

Bonnet A., Haton J.P. and Truong-Ngoc J.M. (1988). *Expert Systems: Principles and Practice*. Prentice-Hall, Englewood Cliffs, NJ.

Booch G. (1990). *Object-Oriented Design*. Benjamin-Cummings. Redwood City, CA.

Buchanan B.G. and Feigenbaum E.A. (1976). Dendral and meta-dendral: their applications dimension. *Artificial Intelligence*, **11**(1), 5–24.

Bramer M.A. (1988). Expert systems in business: a British perspective. *Expert Systems*, **5**(2), 104–117.

Brown A. (1991). *Object-Oriented Databases: Applications in Software Engineering*. McGraw-Hill, London.

Buzan A. (1982). *Use Your Head*. BBC Books, London.

C.C.T.A. (1986). *Expert Systems: Some Guidelines*. London.
Charniak E. and McDermott D. (1985). *Introduction to Artificial Intelligence*. Addison-Wesley, Wokingham.
Chen P.P-S. (1976). The entity–relationship model – toward a unified view of data. *ACM Trans. on Database Systems* **1**(1), 9–36.
Cheung E.L.C. (1989). *Pension Choice: Capturing the Expert's Knowledge*. BSc Computer Studies final year project report, Polytechnic of Wales.
Cutts G. (1991). *Structured Systems Analysis and Design Methodology*, 2nd Edn. Blackwell Scientific, Oxford.
Coad P. and Yourdon E. (1991). *Object-Oriented Analysis*, 2nd Edn. Prentice-Hall, Englewood Cliffs, NJ.
Codd E.F. (1970). A relational model for large shared data banks. *Comm.ACM* **13**(6) 377–387.
Collins H.M. (1990). Knowing and growing: building an expert system for semi-conductor crystal growing. Paper presented at *Social Perspectives of Software – Oxford Workshop*, The Moathouse, 13–14 January.
Dahl O.J., Dijkstra E.W. and Hoare C.A.R. (1972). *Structured Programming*. Academic Press, New York.
Date C.J. (1989). *An Introduction to Database Systems, Vol. 1*, 5th Edn. Addison-Wesley, Reading, MA.
Debenham J.K. (1985). Knowledge base design. *The Australian Computer Journal*, **17**(1), 42–48.
Debenham J.K. (1987). Expert systems: an information processing perspective. In J.Ross Quinlan (Ed.) *Applications of Expert Systems*. Addison-Wesley, Sydney.
De-Marco T. (1979). *Structured Analysis and System Specification*. Prentice-Hall, Englewood Cliffs, NJ.
De Salvo D.A., Glamm A.E. and Liebowitz J. (1987). Structured design of an expert system prototype at the National Archives. In Barry G. Silverman (Ed.) *Expert Systems for Business*. Addison-Wesley, Reading, MA.
Duda R.O. and Gaschnig J.G. (1981). Knowledge-based expert systems come of age. *Byte*. **6**(9), 238–281.
Dreyfus H.L. (1979). *What Computers Can't Do: A Critique of Artificial Reason*. Harper and Row, New York.
Earl M.J. (1989). *Management Strategies for Information Technology*. Prentice-Hall, Hemel Hempstead.
Erman L.D., Hayes-Roth F., Lesser V. and Reddy D. (1980). The HEARSAY-II speech understanding system. Integrating knowledge to resolve uncertainty. *Computing Surveys*, **12**(2), 216–232.
Faden M. (1986). What do you want in a knowledge engineer? *Expert Systems User*, September.
Feigenbaum E.A. (1977). The art of artificial intelligence: themes and case studies of knowledge engineering. *Proc. of 5th International Joint Conf. on Artificial Intelligence*, 1014–1029.
Feigenbaum E.A. and McCorduck P. (1984). *The 5th Generation: Artificial Intelligence and Japan's Computer Challenge to the World*. Michael Joseph, New York.
Finkelstein C. (1989). *An Introduction to Information Engineering: from Strategic Planning to Information Systems*. Addison-Wesley, Sydney.
Forsyth R. (Ed.) (1989). *Expert Systems: Principles and Case Studies*. 2nd Edn. Chapman and Hall, London.
Frost R.A. (1986). *Introduction to Knowledge-Base Systems*. Collins, London.
Gane C. and Sarson T. (1977). *Structured Systems Analysis: Tools and Techniques*. Prentice-Hall, Englewood Cliffs, NJ.
Gaschnig J. (1982). Prospector: an expert system for mineral exploitation. In Bond A. (Ed.) *Machine Intelligence*. Infotech State of the Art Report 9.
Gibson E. (1990). Born and bred: object behaviour analysis. *Byte*, October, 245–254.
Goodall A. (1985). *The Guide to Expert Systems*. Learned Information, Cambridge.
Grover M.D. (1986). A pragmatic knowledge acquisition methodology. *Proc. of 8th International Joint Conf. on Artificial Intelligence*, 436–438.
Harel D. (1988). On visual formalisms. *Comm.ACM*, **31**(5), 514–529.
Hart A.A. (1985). The role of induction in knowledge elicitation. *Expert Systems*, **2**(1), 24–28.
Hart A.A. (1986). *Knowledge Acquisition for Expert Systems*. Kogan Page, London.
Hayball C. and Barlow D. (1990). Skills support in the ICL (Kidsgrove) Bonding Shop – a case study in the application of the KADS methodology. In Berry D. and Hart A. (Eds.) *Expert Systems: Human Aspects*. Chapman and Hall, London.
Hayes-Roth F., Waterman D. and Lenat D.B. (Eds.). (1983). *Building Expert Systems*. Addison-Wesley, Reading, MA.
Hickman F. (Ed.) (1989). *Knowledge Based Systems Analysis: A Pragmatic Introduction to the KADS Methodology*. Ellis Horwood, Cambridge.
Hilal D.K. and Soltan H. (1991). A suggested descriptive framework for the comparison of knowledge-based systems methodologies. *Expert Systems*, **8**(2), 107–114.
Howe D.R. (1983). *Data Analysis for Data Base Design*. Edward Arnold, London.
Humpert B. and Holley P. (1988). Expert systems in finance planning. *Expert Systems*, **5**(2), 78–100.
Jackson P. (1990). *An Introduction to Expert Systems*, 2nd Edn. Addison-Wesley, Reading, MA.
Jarke M. and Vassilou Y. (1984). Coupling expert systems with database management systems. In Reitman W. *Artificial Intelligence Applications for Business*. Ablex Publishing, New York.
Johnson P.E. (1983). What kind of expert system should a system be? *The Journal of Medicine and Philosophy*, **8**, 77–97.
Johnston R. (1986). Early applications get user approval. *Expert Systems User*, November.
Keller R. (1987). *Expert System Technology – Development and Application*. Yourdon Press, New York.

Kerschberg L. (1987a). Expert database systems. *Computer Bulletin*, June.
Kerschberg L. (1987b). *Expert Database Systems: Proc. of 1st International Conf*. Cummins, New York.
King R. (1988). My cat is object-oriented. In Kim W. and Lochovsky F. *Object-Oriented Languages, Applications and Databases*. Addison-Wesley, Reading, MA.
King R. and McLeod D. (1985). Semantic data models. In S.Bing Yao (Ed.) *Principles of Database Design. Vol 1: Logical Organizations*. Prentice-Hall, Englewood Cliffs, NJ.
Klahr P. and Waterman D.A. (Eds.) (1986). *Expert Systems: Techniques, Tools and Applications*. Addison-Wesley, Reading, MA.
Kowalski R. (1984). AI and software engineering. *Datamation*, 3(18), 21–28.
Kung C. (1990). Object subclass hierarchy in SQL: a simple approach. *Comm.ACM*, 33(7), 117–125.
Lehner P.E. and Barth S.W. (1985). Expert systems on micro-computers. *Expert Systems*, 2(4), 12–16.
Liebenau J. and Backhouse J. (1990) *Understanding Information: An Introduction*. Macmillan, London.
Lindsay R.K., Buchanan B.G., Feigenbaum E.A. and Lederburg J. (1980). *Applications of Artificial Intelligence for Organic Chemistry: the DENDRAL Project*. McGraw-Hill, New York.
Maney T. and Reid I. (1986). *A Management Guide to Artificial Intelligence*. Paradigm, London.
Martin J. (1984). *An Information Systems Manifesto*. Prentice-Hall, Englewood Cliffs, NJ.
Martin W.A. and Fateman R.J. (1971). The MACSYMA system. *Proc. of 2nd Symposium on Symbolic and Algebraic Manipulation*, Los Angeles, 59–75.
Martins G.R. (1984). The Overselling of Expert Systems. *Datamation*. 3(18), 31–32.
McCorduck P. (1978). *Machines Who Think*. Freeman and Co, New York.
McDermott J. (1980). R1: an expert in the computer systems domain. *Proc of American Association for AI Conf*.
Minsky M. (1975). A framework for representing knowledge. In Winston P.H. (Ed.). *The Psychology of Computer Vision*. McGraw-Hill, New York.
Mylopoulos J. (1989). On knowledge base management systems. In Mylopoulos J. and Brodie M. *Readings in AI and Database Systems*. Morgan Kauffmann, New York.
Mylopoulos J., Borgida A., Jarke M. and Koubarakis M. (1990). Telos:representing knowledge about information systems. *ACM Trans. on Information Systems*, 8(4), 325–362.
Mumford E. (1985). *Knowledge Engineering, Expert Systems and Organizational Change*. Working Paper, Manchester Business School.
Newquist H.P. (1990). Experts at retail. *Datamation*, April, 53–56.
Nilsson N.J. (1982). *Principles of Artificial Intelligence*. Tioga, Palo Alto, CA.
Olson J.R. and Reuter H.H. (1987). Extracting expertise from experts: methods for knowledge acquisition. *Expert Systems*, 4(3), 152–168.
Popolizio J.J. and Capelli W.S. (1989). New shells for old iron. *Datamation*, April, 41–48.
Porter M.E. (1985). *Competitive Advantage: Creating and Sustaining Superior Performance*. Free Press, New York.
Preece A.D. (1990). Towards a methodology for evaluating expert systems. *Expert Systems*, 7(4), 215–223.
Quinlan J.R. (1979). Discovering rules by induction from large collections of examples. In Michie D. (Ed.) *Expert Systems in the Micro-Electronic Age*. Edinburgh University Press, 168–201.
Reitman W. (1984). *Artificial Intelligence Applications for Business*. Ablex Publishing, New York.
Rich E. (1983). *Artificial Intelligence*. McGraw-Hill, New York.
Searle J.R. (1986). *Minds, Brains and Science*. Harvard University Press.
Schafer D.G. (1985). Micro-computer based expert systems: where are we, where are we headed. *Expert Systems*, 2(4), 95–102.
Shortliffe E.H. (1976). *Computer-Based Medical Consultations: MYCIN*. Elsevier, New York.
Silverman B.G. (Ed.) (1987). *Expert Systems for Business*. Addison-Wesley, Reading, MA.
Simon H.A. (1969). *The Sciences of the Artificial*. MIT Press, Cambridge, MA.
Simon H.A. (1977). *The New Science of Management Decision*. Prentice-Hall, Englewood Cliffs, NJ.
Smith J.M. and Smith D.C.P. (1976). Database abstractions: aggregation and generalization. *ACM Trans. on Database Systems* 2(2), 105–133.
Sowa J.F. (1984). *Conceptual Structures: Information Processing in Mind and Machine*. Addison-Wesley. Reading, MA.
Stonebraker M. and Rowe L.A. (1985). *The Design of Postgres*. Memorandum, Electronics Research Laboratory, University of California, Berkeley.
Stamper R.K. (1973). *Information in Business and Administrative Systems*. Batsford, London.
Stamper R.K. (1985). Information: mystical fluid or a subject for scientific enquiry? *The Computer Journal*, 28(3), 195–156.
Stow R., Lunn S. and Slatter P. (1988). How to identify business applications of expert systems. *2nd International Expert Systems Conference*, Brighton.
Suen C., Grogono P., Shinghal R. and Coallier F. (1990). Verifying, validating and measuring performance of expert systems. *Expert System with Applications*, 1(2), 93–102.
Sviokla J. (1986). Business implications of knowledge-based systems. *Database*, Summer and Fall.

Swaffield G. and Knight B. (1990). Applying systems analysis techniques to knowledge engineering. *Expert Systems*, **7**(2), 82–93.

Teorey T.J., Yang D. and Fry J.P. (1986). A logical design methodology for relational databases using the extended entity–relationship model. *ACM Computing Surveys*, **18**, 197–222.

Thompson B. and Thompson W. (1986). Finding rules in data. *Byte*, November.

Tsichritzis D.C. and Lochovsky F.H. (1982). *Data Models*. Prentice-Hall, Englewood Cliffs, NJ.

Van Melle W., Shortliffe E.H. and Buchanan B.G. (1981). EMYCIN: a domain independent system that aids in constructing knowledge based consultation programs. *Machine Intelligence*. Infotech State of the Art Report 9.

Verheijen G.M.A. and Van Bekkum J. (1982). NIAM: an information analysis method. In Olle T.W. and Sol H.G. (Eds.) *Information Systems Design Methodologies: A Comparative Review*. North Holland, Amsterdam.

Waterman D.A. (1986). *A Guide to Expert Systems*. Addison-Wesley, Reading, MA.

Weilinga B.J. and Breuker J.A. (1986). Models of expertise. *7th European Conference on AI, Vol 1*. Brighton, July.

Weizenbaum J. (1976). *Computer Power and Human Reason*. Freeman and Co, New York.

Wellbank M. (1983). *A Review of Knowledge Acquisition Techniques for Expert Systems*. British Telecom Research Laboratories, Martlesham Heath, Ipswich, England.

White I. (1987). W(h)ither expert systems. *BCS Specialist Group on Expert Systems, Newsletter*, 17.

Winograd T. and Flores F. (1986). *Understanding Computers and Cognition: A New Foundation for Design*. Ablex Publishing, Norwood, NJ.

Winston P.H. (1984). *Artificial Intelligence*. Addison-Wesley, Reading, MA.

Winston P.H. and Prendergast K.A. (Eds.) (1984). *The AI Business: the Commercial Uses of Artificial Intelligence*. MIT Press, Cambridge, MA.

Yourdon E. and Constantine L.L. (1977). *Structured Design*, 2nd Edn. Yourdon Press.

Yourdon E. (1990). Auld Lang Syne. *Byte*, October, 257–261.

INDEX